COME CLOSER TO YOURSELF

From Lorraine Phelan

March 2016

COME CLOSER TO YOURSELF

Angela Josephine

M.G. NEELS

authorHOUSE®

AuthorHouse™ UK Ltd.
1663 Liberty Drive
Bloomington, IN 47403 USA
www.authorhouse.co.uk
Phone: 0800.197.4150

© 2013 by M.G. NEELS. All rights reserved.

No part of this book may be reproduced, stored
in a retrieval system, or transmitted by any means
without the written permission of the author.

Published by AuthorHouse 09/11/2013

ISBN: 978-1-4918-7613-8 (sc)
ISBN: 978-1-4918-7614-5 (e)

Library of Congress Control Number: 2013915151

Any people depicted in stock imagery provided by Thinkstock are models,
and such images are being used for illustrative purposes only.
Certain stock imagery © Thinkstock.

This book is printed on acid-free paper.

Because of the dynamic nature of the Internet, any web addresses or links contained in this book may have changed since publication and may no longer be valid. The views expressed in this work are solely those of the author and do not necessarily reflect the views of the publisher, and the publisher hereby disclaims any responsibility for them.

CONTENTS

INTRODUCTION vii

YOUR DEEPEST LONGING 1

THE WONDER OF YOUR BEING 9

YOUR LIFE'S JOURNEY 23

WHAT DO YOU EXIST FOR ? 29

THE GROUND ON WHICH YOU STAND 36

WHO IS YOUR MODEL OR MENTOR ? 47

HOW DO YOU STAND IN THE WORLD ? 53

YOU ARE CALLED TO BE FREE 61

THE TRUTH SETS YOU FREE 75

STANDING IN YOUR TRUTH 82

LIVING IN THE HERE AND NOW 90

BEING LIKE A CHILD 100

LIVING IN EXPECTANCY 105

RECONCILED WITH DYING 110

BY WAY OF CONCLUDING 120

INTRODUCTION

Being closer to yourself : isn't that something you long for at times ? Life can be so hectic. Whether you are a parent, a teacher, a devoted social worker, or a dedicated member of the clergy or of a religious order, the rhythm of life absorbs you inexorably. Often you merely drive on your automatic pilot. It may be, though, that you already took the habit of just being with yourself for a short time at regular intervals. If so, you have experienced that this gives you a feeling of freedom and opens up an inner space of peace.

What would you think of taking a few days off so as to come closer to yourself ? You don't even have to leave your home for that. You could well choose a day every other week that would be entirely yours. Still, you perhaps know people who withdraw from their current occupations for a few days in an abbey or some quiet nature spot, so as to seek the silence and touch into the deeper layers of themselves. In the Catholic tradition, clergy and consecrated persons have the luxury of doing that for a week or so each year. They call it « making their retreat ».

What do these people do all day when they 'make a retreat'? And suppose you would have the opportunity of isolating yourself for a week or so, how would you spend the time ? You could walk about in silence, seeking to consciously come into contact with the mystery of your being and of the world around you. That is salutary indeed. But you could hardly do that all day long. People who withdraw into the silence of a monastery often look for a good spiritual book that can help them reflect on the quality of their life.

I wish to hand you such a book. Its main purpose is not to shower you with lots of spiritual ideas, though they obviously are not absent from the book. Rather it aims at proposing concrete exercises for you to do during that peaceful time you set apart for yourself. Those exercises aim at helping you to ask yourself some important questions for your growth in authentic humanity, for, as Iraeneus, an early Christian writer, wrote : « The Glory of God is the human person fully alive ». Some of these exercises are inspired by the Jewish and Christian sacred writings, others are simply psychological. They complete each other. For, a genuine spiritual life is lived not so much in beautiful ideas, but in and through the stirrings of our body and psyche.

This book offers you several themes that concern your genuine Self. Obviously, you must feel free to choose any one of these that immediately appeals to you when browsing through the table of contents. However, these themes are inter-connected in such a way that each theme builds further on the previous one. It is, therefore, advisable to follow the sequence of the themes. In this way you may even find that you have material for more days to come than you thought at first. At any rate, it is important that you remain with a particular theme as long as you feel that it inspires and enlightens you. It is more helpful to allow a particular facet of your life to seep in than to want to deal with all of them right away.

Perhaps you may find material here that can help you listen to yourself in a mere half an hour a day, to allow yourself to be questioned by the divine spark that kindles you and that so much wants to inspire your entire personality and your concrete way of living. The considerations and exercises offered here are only doors that can be opened so as to enter into your Self. Perhaps you simply wish to try and open one or two of them. You will be astonished at what you may find behind that door.

Keep a notebook close at hand for you to write down what you experience during an exercise : what insights you gain, what emotions or feelings you have, which invitations you receive, what challenges present themselves to you. That can help you to come as close to yourself as possible. And it will provide you with an opportunity for returning at a later moment to some insights that were particularly beneficial for you.

YOUR DEEPEST LONGING

From your early years onward, you have been told that you have to achieve something with your life, that you need to realize something useful and succeed in it. You believed this and applied it to your personal development as well as to the tasks you took upon yourself.

You must achieve something : that is partially true and valuable, for, ultimately, we carry the responsibility for the quality of our life. Still, this way of conceiving life is basically flawed. It sounds as if we ourselves are able to determine and effectuate what our life is to be. While, in fact, life is more a matter of being gifted with and by Life, of allowing life to happen to us and through us. And yet all of us repeatedly put to ourselves the question : what must I do now ? What is expected of me ? In what direction do I have to move ? Which road should I take ?

Just as your living organism is kept alive by your precious breath, in much the same way the 'Breath of God'—the biblical name for what we currently call the divine Spirit—operates in the depth of yourself so as to lead your life ahead. How can you touch into that deep inner guidance ? For that, I think, you need as much as possible come in touch with your deepest authentic longing : what is it you want above all, what do you desire most deeply ? Is it not significant that the only question Jesus put to the first two of his future disciples who approached him hesitantly, was : « What is it you want ? » They had tried things out first with John the Baptist, but they had felt an inner urge to turn to Jesus instead, and that was the first thing they heard from his mouth : « What is it you want ? » (John 1, 35-39)

Something deep within us drives us on. There is a kind of current in us that wants to flow and that manifests itself in all kinds of desires calling to be fulfilled. It is important to be in touch with that inner energy. What is your soul searching for ? What is its deepest longing ? It is of vital importance to become conscious of that, because our deepest longing is precisely the place where we can touch into the creative Spirit, the spot where the Spirit wants to reach us and guide us. Your deepest longing is the reflection of the divine dimension of your being. In his book 'Experiencing God', Anselm Grün says beautifully : « God let the anchor of longing down into our soul so that we may be able to berth. »

It isn't that easy to come into contact with our deepest desire, for we have so many desires looking for gratification that burn a good deal of our energy. And it happens quite often that, pushed by this or that desire, we pursue someone or something, thinking that thereby we will find fulfillment, only to find afterwards that we have been pursuing an illusion. And we feel cheated. No wonder : we have substituted a mere desire (with a small 'd') for our Desire (with a capital 'D').

In his book, Anselm Grün narrates how the German poet Raine Maria Rilke imagines that God, before sending a new human being into the world, gives him/her a word for the road. The word is : « Sent forth by your senses, go to the very edge of your longing : give it a form ». The poet calls us to go unto the frontiers of our longing so that it may raise us above this world. I do not feel quite at ease with that expression 'Raising us beyond this world', for our task is precisely to realise our personal calling *in* this world. In one of his other poems Rilke wrote : « This is The Longing : to inhabit the swell and not make one's home in Time. »

To lodge in the swell ? That's not very pleasant and a bit shaky ; we would rather be cosy at home ! And even when we are willing to move with the swell, we still desire to ultimately reach home, to be home. All our activities, all our searchings are, all things considered, but an effort to assuage that longing for 'being at home'. And in order to 'come home', we jump from one desire to another !

Perhaps we need to call lots of those desires by their true name : they simply are cravings. There is nothing fundamentally wrong with craving for something. Only do we need to realize that those desires give us the illusion that their fulfillment is the answer to our deepest longing. A desire is nothing but a distorted reflection of our true Desire. In it we hope to find what we long for in the depth of our heart. But we do not pay attention to that inner longing itself. In fact, with that desire we pass by our Longing. We make ourselves dependent on something which seems to hold the promise of giving us what our heart desires. But is doesn't.

Don't we all have desires that make us dependent but do not get us any further ? Hopefully we do not try to assuage our longing with drink or drugs—that would be disastrous. Yet we see it happening all the time around us. But there also exists something like dependence on work. Or compulsive seeking recognition so as to feel worthwhile. Or maintaining a passionate relationship in order to feel lovable.

Perhaps we were taught that desires are wrong or at least dangerous, that we need to fight against them or be ashamed of them. Did one not all too easily speak of 'sinful desires' ? Would it not be more beneficial to focus our attention on our soul, and to find and recognize in those desires our deeply buried Desire at work ?

Hence my question : what is your deepest Desire ? Of course, you cannot answer this question in a blink of an eye. And surely not by racking your brain. It is something you need to listen to within yourself. When, in stillness, you put that question to your soul, you are tuning in to the wavelength of the divine, for it is the desire of your Creator that you live to the full. Hence, when you question your heart about its deepest desire, you will discover how best to respond to the Creator's desire for you.

Entering into silence so as to touch into your deep desire, you are in fact in 'prayer' in the most genuine meaning of that word. For what is prayer ? Anselm Grün tells us that, according to Saint-Augustine, abiding in your deepest desire is already prayer. In his commentary on the psalm 25 Augustine writes : « Your desire *is* your prayer. And if your desire is constant, then your prayer is continuous ! Your uninterrupted desire is your uninterrupted voice of prayer ». Hence, touching into the deepest desire present in the depth of your heart, is praying in the true sens of the word, for that desire already unites us with God. The French edition of the Catholic Breviary uses a marvelous phrase for this in one of its hymns : « Tu nous manques, Seigneur ; dans le tréfonds de notre cœur ta place reste marquée comme un grand vide, une blessure », which means : «We miss you, Lord. In the depth of our heart your place is marked by a great void, a wound ». And we have to keep this place open, else we will run aground in all sorts of desires that will prevent us from living to the full. Hence it is important not to think of prayer as cultivating nice religious ideas, feelings or formula, but rather as coming in touch with The Longing that is alive in us and that wants to lead our life's energy into the right direction.

The purpose of this reflection is not so much that you agree theoretically with what is said here, but that you try to come into contact with your Desire and learn to abide with it. Perhaps the following exercises may help you do that.

Exercise 1 :

Go to a quiet place to either walk or sit undisturbed, and ask yourself : What is my deepest Desire ? Don't think too much—this is not an exam—but listen to the spontaneous response of your soul. You need to be in deep stillness for this. It may take some time to find the answer. Words and images will pop up in your mind, probably a number of them, so that you will not so quickly know which is the main desire that inhabits you. Note whatever emerges in you. Decide then which desire your heart can most identify itself with.

Exercise 2 :

Or, again in quiet spot, make a list of your most frequent desires, whether they are material or psychological or even spiritual—for we look for fulfilment in all three of these areas.

Now have a close look at each one in turn of the desires you noted and ask : « What hides behind this desire ? Can I go one layer deeper and see whether there is not a deeper desire hiding behind this one » ? It is likely that you will have to descend a few layers before you hit on your most basic desire.

When you realize that you can descend no more and you think you have reached the most basic desire, give it a name that expresses what possibly is your deepest longing. Stay with it then for a while so as to acknowledge it fully.

Exercise 3 :

In case you live in the Jewish-Christian tradition, ponder on a Bible passage that looks like your deepest longing. For example : Psalm 63, 1-9 ; Psalm 84 ; Psalm 42, 1-3 ; or Isaiah 26, 9

THE WONDER OF YOUR BEING

What is the most precious thing you own ?

Do not read further right now but pause in a quiet place, with a listening heart. And put to yourself that question : « What is the most precious thing I have? » Probably the answer will not present itself so quickly, but simply continue to listen. And note what emerges in you.

You may now read further.

As for me, I think that the most precious thing I have my own self is, my own being. My life. Perhaps you feel the same way? Every human being is a miracle. One of the Jewish prayers says : « Ah, what is man that you should spare a thought for him, the son of man that you should care for him. Yet, you have made him little less than a god, you have crowned him with glory and splendour. » (Ps. 8) Do you believe that this verse speaks about you ? If so, take a few moments to stay with these words ; let them seep into you.

And how do you feel about that ? Do you like yourself ? Do you esteem your own worth ?

That is not self-evident. Often you think and dream and act of an idealized image of yourself and not from within your genuine Self. Your educators made you believe that you had to be and act in such a way or another, in order to be acceptable and lovable. And you spent quite some energy in trying to be the one they wanted you to be, or you yourself thought you had to be so as to be worthwhile.

You did that frequently—and perhaps you still do—instead of simply being the person you are divinely called to be. For you are so valuable, so lovable, simply because you *are.* For you are a unique human person among six billion others. You are unique. No other person is exactly like you. In one of his books Anselm Grün says : « God wants to pronounce something into this world that He can only make known by me, as I have been made and have become. Each human person is unique. He or she is an image of that which God desired for him or her. And my calling is to allow that unique particular image of God to shine forth in this world. » (Bilder von Jesus, 2001, p. 146)

You have been called into existence so that you may simply become what you are supposed to be : your unique, specific, individual (but not individualistic) Self. Hence you do not at all need to come up to the ideal self you dream of being or that others expect you to be. You do not need to produce anything. All that fretting about becoming this or that, is simply affectation by your 'I '(Ego). You have a deeper, more precious kernel by which you are called to live, each day anew. It is divine.

But that supposes that you first receive and accept yourself as you have been created. And that you believe in that benevolent life-force that wants to flow in you. You are a spark of the Light that God is, a spark that has to shine in this or that way and not another. You are a crystal in which the divine light wants to be seen in a multicoloured reflection. I read in one of Anselm Grün's books a beautiful poem by Magdalena Robben :

> *~ I dreamt that since ancient times I have been searching.—I am searching for a crystal.—I land into a cavern, and I climb a mountain—I search in the sea and fly in the sky.—I rush from place to place, day after day.—Torn by my craving.—Torn by my search.—Until I drop exhausted to the ground.*

> ~ Crisis—creative jump.—The earth catches me.—The wind cools my body soaked in sweat.—The grass caresses me softly.—I smell the recently cut grass.—I see a dandelion in the lightness of her being.—She smiles at me.
>
> ~ Then I hear a whisper, a voice in me :—What are you looking for here ? What do you seek?—Never forget : the crystal is inside you.—And I woke up.

Awaken to the consciousness that you are a crystal. The sand on the shore consists of billions of crystals, and each one of them is different. The snowflakes whirling past your window consist of billions of crystals and each one of them is different. Our planet is inhabited by more than six billion people and each one of them is different. So, you have your own unique worth and beauty. Can you feel astonished at that ? Can you be in admiration for it ? In his book 'Confessions' (X-8), Saint Augustine wrote : « People continue to be astonished at the hight of mountains, at the enormous waves of the sea, at the breadth of rivers, at the extent of the oceans and the trajectories of stars, but they pass themselves by without ever being astonished. »

Spend some time now in admiration for the unique precious being you are. It is exactly as this unique being that you are valued and unconditionally loved by God/The Universe/The Ground of all being. You do not need to prove anything, neither to God nor to anybody else, not even to yourself. You may simply be. Do you believe that ?

Browse a moment through the set of exercises that follow. See which exercises appeal most to you. Choose them and start doing them now.

Exercise 1

Lie down on your back, or sit straight in a chair with your two feet firmly on the ground. Direct your attention to each part of your body in turn, starting from your toes up to your crown, each time letting go of all tension in the part you are directing your attention to.

Now allow your breathing to slow down and feel your breath travelling from your lower abdomen to the top of your lungs and back. Give your attention entirely to the entering and leaving of the air : pure, cold air traveling up your nose so as to charge your bloodstream with oxygen, and foul, warm air being expelled. This is your life's stream, ever since your first cry on leaving your mother's womb. How many years, how many times a minute, has this vitalizing breath entered you ? What a wonder that is !

Call a moment to mind that symbol of the Book of Origins in the Bible (Genesis 2, 7) : « Then God fashioned the human being from the soil . . . and He blew breath into his nose. Thus man became a living being. » Every single moment you are *becoming* a living being ; you can't accomplish this yourself. And every so many seconds you breathe, you do not invent that either. You may live, totally free and for nothing ! Let this get through to you . . .

Exercise 2

Lie down on your back on the floor or on your bed. Direct your attention to all the functions of your body, to each one in turn. Beware : to be truly present to that bodily function is not the same as thinking about it : *feel* your organism. Allow yourself to be touched by the wonder of each bodily function and value it :

~ Become aware of your skeleton : the marvelous structure and flexibility of your spine and of all your bones. Make a few movements with your arms and legs and admire the way they all fit together.

~ now become aware of your set of muscles : visit them one by one, starting from your toes upwards. Tighten and relax each muscle. Admire the ingenuity of that organism.

~ now become aware of your heartbeat : how many years already, how many times a minute, does this mighty muscle pump blood through your arteries so as to carry oxygen to your furthest tissues ? Be in admiration for the discreet, uninterrupted and faithful service of this wonderful organ.

~ now direct your attention toward your abdomen with its ingenuous systems of absorption, transformation and elimination of foodstuffs : that entire complex system of feeding, allowing the billions of cells in your body to be constantly renewed.

~ finally, take some time to be with your sexual organs, the beauty of your manliness or womanhood.

« And God saw that it was good, yes, very good indeed », says the Jewish Bible (Gen. 1, 31). Do you agree ? Do you feel that way ?

When you finish this long visit of your wonderful organism, sit back and wonder how harmoniously every part of that super-intelligent complexity operates and gives you that wonderful feeling, in and through your body, of being a *living* being. You tend to take it all for granted, but is it a matter of course ? Can you feel the marvel of it all ?

Exercise 3

Go and take a quiet walk in the natural world and become aware of the miracle of your senses :

~ your *eyes* : look for a while intensely at the light, the variety of forms and colours. Do it without reasoning or analyzing : just look ! Take it in ! Allow the wonder of it all to reach you. Feel grateful that you can see . . .

~ your *ears* : listen attentively to the many sounds that reach you. Do not analyze or name them : just let the wonder of sound reach you. And feel grateful that you can hear . . .

~ your *voice* : make a prolonged sound (aaaaa . . . ooooo . . . .) or sing a melody you cherish and listen to the beauty of its sound. Allow yourself to be amazed by it.

~ your *sense of smell* : becomes aware of the fragrances around you ; smell different flowers you meet on your walk. Feel grateful that you can smell . . .

~ your *taste* : pick up a fruit or take a sweet. Let is slowly melt in your mouth and take the time to enjoy the taste of it. Feel grateful for the gift of taste . . .

Come Closer to Yourself

~ your sense of *touch* : pay attention to the breeze caressing your face or the warmth of the sun on your skin. Gently stroke your bare arms and feel their sensitivity. Touch for a while a tree, a leaf, a beautiful object, a pet. Feel grateful for the sense of touch . . .

All your senses are instruments of exchange with the universe, with all that exists and lives around you. Every sense experience enriches you, ennobles your life. Is all that a matter of course ? Can you marvel at it ? And be full of admiration ?

Exercise 4

Take a seat in a spot where you cannot be disturbed. Take time to be with that mysterious part of yourself we call our soul or our spirit or our consciousness, which enables you to reach out and communicate beyond the physical boundaries of your senses.

~ Become aware of your *mind* : you are able to penetrate the nature and meaning of things ; you can make connections between various insights, you can query and examine difficult matters. Become aware of a field of knowledge that is important to you and you are familiar with, and gratefully realize how it has enriched you. And remain now for a while in gratitude for all the fields of interest you can cover . . .

~ Become aware of your *memory* : you are able to recall earlier experiences and bring them as it were back to the present. Now recall a particularly happy experience of your life and stay with it for a while, tasting anew something of the contentment that you then felt. And feel happy that you have this capacity of reviving moments of joy of the past . . .

~ Become aware of your *imagination* : you can call to mind persons and places, and see them with the eye of your mind as if they were physically present. You also can create newness with your fantasy and paint beautiful inner pictures. Take a few moments to make a trip to a fantasy world and admire the fact that this is even possible !

~ Become aware of your *affectivity* : you are able to feel affection for people, whether alive or deceased, whom you love or are loved by, and this beyond the physical boundaries even of other continents ! Take a few moments to abide with the affection you feel for a beloved person who is far away and yet whose friendship you can experience right here and now. Feel the joy of that feeling of connectedness and marvel at the fact that this is at all possible beyond the boundaries of place and time . . .

Exercise 5

Take a seat somewhere quiet and where you can take notes.

~ Make a list of your talents and skills, be they artistic, practical, technical, relational, intellectual, educational, social, organisational, etc. Stay now with a few of these that make you happy to have them, and feel grateful for the fact that they are to be found within you . . . free of charge !

~ Recall some instances or places where some of these talents of yours made a person or a group of people happier, richer, freer. Your talents are first and foremost a gift to yourself, but to the extent that you make use of them unselfishly and gratefully, they automatically become channels of enrichment for others. Be conscious of the fact that you become an instrument of enrichment for others when you do not belittle yourself but make positive use of your giftedness.

Exercise 6

If you are part of the Jewish-Christian tradition, you might take your Bible and find a quiet spot where to read and savour some passage that expresses that priceless gift of who you are. You have been gifted with yourself, all is gift to you, for you could not and cannot create yourself, you originate from an ever flowing, never ceasing source.

For example :

Psalm 139, verses 1 to 6, 13 to 16 ; Genesis 2, 7-8 (be conscious of it that this is happening to you, now !) ; Isaiah 43, 1-7 ; Jesus Sirach (Ecclesiastes) 17, 1-10 ; Acts of the Apostles 17, 28.

Exercise 7

In the intimacy of your bedroom, take a seat in front of a mirror. In it :

~ Look into your eyes, without speaking, with an open heart, with a quiet gaze.

~ Now say with all the warmth you are capable of : I like you, it is good that you are there, I love you !

~ Gently pronounce your first name. Which name does God love here: the one I see in the mirror or some other me I dream of ?

~ Should you not feel able to speak these words, then ask yourself : what is it that prevents me from saying this wholeheartedly ? What prevents me from liking myself ?

Come Closer to Yourself

~ Prayerfully now say what you truly feel about the gift that you are and that your Creator esteems to be « very good » (Genesis 1, 31).

In case you find it too threatening to do this exercise in front of a mirror, try it with a photograph of yourself. It comes down to the same thing, although a picture is often somewhat idealized. A mirror shows you the person you are here and now. Can you say to *this* person : I love you ? Do not forget : there is Someone who can and does say it, always !

Exercise 8

The mystery of your existence unfolds itself from within an inner core the nature of which we cannot truly know nor describe. Yet, we do know very well that all that is alive in us is set in motion and is directed by « something-somewhere-inside-you ». We perhaps call it our « soul ». We can express that inner core of ourselves by symbols only. Different cultures and religions did present us with such symbols. Do you have a symbol of your 'soul' which you find expressive ?

~ It may be a symbol borrowed from nature : a sun, a star, a fire, a bubbling source, a rose, a lotusflower, a jewel, a crystal which reflects the light, a precious pearl, a seed that is on the point of sprouting . . .

~ For some people a geometrical figure is very significant : a circle, a globe, an equilateral triangle, a mandala . . .

~ Others prefer a personification : an angel of light, an inner teacher, an old sage, an inner child, the Buddha, the inner Christ . . .

Have a look at what symbol appeals to you for expressing the ineffable nature of your unique and precious Self. For some time, first contemplate that symbol from the outside as it were, in your imagination, and ask it what it wishes to express about your precious Self. Then imagine that this symbol enters into you and situates itself in the centre of yourself. Stay with it there for a while and note whatever emerges inside you . . .

If each day you do just one of these exercises, within a week's time you will have come closer to yourself!

YOUR LIFE'S JOURNEY

Your being is a marvel. You are a living creature. Free of charge you have been given to yourself so as to live that unique life of yours to the full. And you may do this as the unique person you are. Therefore, your existence implies an assignment that is specifically yours. Like a seed that had to grow, your unique calling was deposited in you since your birth. Slowly it had to germinate and come up. For that you received time, for life happens in time. In fact, some beautiful things that were expressions of your personal vocation have already happened in your life. But there were also moments and instances that frustrated your life's assignment because you yourself or others interpreted it wrongly. Still, you surely want to give yourself the opportunity to become the person you are called to be?

The past phases of your life can teach you something about that. The manner in which you live your life these days is being influenced by the developments that took place in the earlier periods of your life. And the way you will give meaning and direction to the years still to come, will be influenced by the way you feel about your life right now. So, I invite you to take some time now to look back upon your past history. How do you now feel about the past phases of your life that were granted to you ? You have made quite a journey already. You experienced pain and joy, prosperity and setbacks, mistakes and successes, disappointments and achievements. Theoretically you know that all this is inevitably part of a person's history, but how was that for *your* pilgrimage in life ? Did you become the one you are called to be ? If you are willing to consider this question now, let it not be in order to evaluate your life, to draw up a balance sheet, and still less to judge or condemn it, but simply to marvel at it. To wonder at the subtle manner in which your authentic individuality tried to find its way over the years. To wonder so as to admire. Yes, admire how your unique soul that carries the Creator's desire for you, faithfully made an effort to guide your life in the right direction. It did not let you down ! There were probably moments in your life that you now label as negative, and it is even possible that things you went through are still making too big an impression on you, so that you feel unable to fully appreciate the gift of your own life's development. Of course you suffered at times. Obviously, you sometimes made mistakes. Naturally, some people made it difficult for you to be the person you truly are. But did your personal calling nevertheless not try to find its way within you ? And notice, not *in spite of* those difficulties, but precisely *because of* those difficulties or setbacks. Can you recognize that a golden thread runs through your history ? How gifted and graced you have been, always anew ?

In case you are well acquainted with the Bible, you must have noticed how its different books want to tell the story of God's deepest desire for humanity, and how people repeatedly ignored that divine desire, and how God then had to enliven people's awareness of it again and again ? You read there how periods in which people in their stupidity or arrogance did not listen to God, alternated with periods in which they repented and again heard God's desire for their human existence to be happy. At a certain moment Moses admonished the people not to forget its own history so as to remain lucid : « But take care what you do and be on your guard. Do not forget the things your eyes have seen, nor let them slip from your heart all the days of your life. » (Dt. 4, 9) By calling to mind their earlier experiences, the people could hold on more easily to God's purpose for them. Is that not similarly the case for you and me ? Every human person has his/her history of well-being and calamity. Becoming more aware of how that was for you, you will be more able to be on the wavelength of God's desire that inhabits you and wants to lead you on. Have a try at charting your personal history, as the psalm says : «Remembering God's achievements, remembering your marvels in the past, I reflect on all that you did, I ponder on all your achievements. » (Psalm 77, 11)

Exercise 1

In former times—and still these days—people used to make the pilgrimage on foot to Santiago de Compostella in Spain. Obviously the journey had to be made in different stages. Small chapels and shelters demarcated those stages. Each leg of the journey was an experience of its own.

Go and sit in a place where you will not be easily interrupted, and consider your own history as a journey in different stages. Which were the major phases of your trip ? Recall the places and persons that were a gift to you on your trip. Who and what enriched you, affirmed you, redeemed you, enriched you then ? Let admiration and gratitude rise up in you as you remember all the good things that befell you on your way . . .

Recall in this manner the main turning points of your life's development : when and how a previous stage was closed and a new one began, and ask yourself what was the specific gift of each phase for you. Until you arrive at the present place you are in. And be conscious of its present gift to you.

Exercise 2

Take a large sheet of paper and trace on it the course of your life in the form of a river. Mark the place where it originated, and then paint the manner in which it slowly found its way in the landscape of your existence : how at times it had to force a passage for itself through rocky parts, at other times had to make a new channel for itself because of a dam that had been put up, became a swamp for a while or partially dried up, had to make a couple of big bends in its course, ran at times smoothly in an open plane, or advanced in cascades in a more mountanous area . . .

Use a blue pencil to trace the meandering course of the river of your life, and use other colours for the different parts of the landscape so as to symbolize the mood of this or that period. Write names of places and significant persons and dates here and there along the stream. And as you now get in touch with all these memories, recognize how, notwithstanding its unexpected turns, that stream has carried you along without you ever drowning . And feel grateful for your safe and often pleasant life's journey.

Exercise 3

In case you made one or two of the previous exercises, ask yourself : how did I earn this ? We often put that question when we are faced with trials but seldom when we have a pleasant experience ! In that case we only find it a matter of course that things always turn out for the best !

Allow yourself to be touched by the fact that all those gifts of your life were totally free of charge : they happened to you, they simply occurred and took place and were given to you. That was the concrete way of your 'being created' ! Who or what lies at the base of your life ? A free and generous initiative somehow, that constantly gives further and new life, that enhances it, heals it, enriches it, by means of a series of dear people and positive energies . . .

Exercise 4

Perhaps you may find this reflected in one or another Bible passage. For instance :

~ Isaiah 40, 27-31 ; 41, 8-14 ; 43, 1-5a ; 46, 3-4 and 9-10

~ Dt 8, 2-6 ; Psalm 23 or 103 ; Letter to the Hebrews 11, 8-10 and 13-16

WHAT DO YOU EXIST FOR ?

Do we need a reason for existing ?

Why do I pose such a question ? Do we not all want to be useful for something or someone ? And do people not ask us once in a while : « what do you do in life ? » It looks as if they think that you exist in order to do something, to be useful, to achieve something. In an article written in a Dutch periodical by Ann Verscuren she tells us that at times people ask her what she is doing in life. By which they mean, of course, how she is making a living. My usual answer, she says, is : « I breathe . » And, of course, people then look at me as if I had walked straight out of an asylum. You, too, probably think : what kind of an answer is this !? Perhaps you find it normal that you identify yourself with a particular task which you think is making your life meaningful. Anyhow, did I myself not say, in the previous chapter of this book, that each one of us has a personal calling or 'vocation'? Something that, since our birth, lies waiting to sprout in us, as a kind of expectation of some life assignment to be realized ? What sense does it make, then, to ask what we exist for ? Does breathing suffice ?!

Still, ask a tree what it is standing there for. What its use is. You certainly have an opinion about that : it is there to offer its shade for you to sit in, or to adorn your garden, or to offer its wood to make furniture or at least firewood. But suppose your tree would be able to talk. It would probably tell you that all your considerations are but projections on your part, that it is standing there simply to be there, just like that, in all its beauty which it did not invent itself. It is standing there because it exists. And it is standing there in a good spot—for look how it blossoms !—even if you think that it would better stand somewhere else, so as to stand out better !

In one of her collection of poems, the famous Polish poet Wislawa Zymborska published a poem called 'Hommage to a small self-conceit', and it goes like this —in my poor attempt at translation:

> *The buzzard has nothing to reproach himself for.—Scruples are unfamiliar to the black panther—Piranhas don't doubt as to whether their deeds are lawful—The rattlesnake accepts himself without reservation—Self-critical jackals*

are non-existent—Grasshoppers, caimen, worms, hornets live as they live and are happy that way—The heart of a swordfish weights a hundred kilos, but from another point of view it is light—Nothing is more animal than a clear conscience on the third planet of the sun.

After all, is it not similar for you and me ? What is the aim or purpose of your life ? That you live ! That you exist ! The sense of your life is that you are here and may live. Just like that. As you are. One day, when visiting a old lady in Germany, she gave me an pretty object in glass in which these words were engraved : « Schön dass es dich gibt », which means : Nice that you exist ! That message for me stands for ever in my prayer corner ! People may project expectations onto us, and perhaps we do this ourselves and think that we would stand out better somewhere else. If we would be more intelligent, if we would be more attractive, if our breasts were bigger, if we . . . If, if, if . . . All this results in a loss of energy, for you simply are who you are, here, at this moment of history and on this spot of our planet. Is that not enough ? What dreamers we are and indulgers in all kinds of fancies ! As if being yourself would not be enough !

We are touching a very important point here : the fact of the totally uncalled-for character of our existence, of the free gift of our life that should fill us with immense joy. If you would be able to fully accept being who you are, would not all kinds of good things happen to you uncalled-for and befall others because of you ?

In the French edition of the Catholic book of monastic prayer, I find a hymn which I like very much because it expresses that so beautifully :

> En toute vie, le silence dit Dieu—*In all life the silence speaks of God*
>
> Tout ce qui est tressaille d'être à Lui—*All that exists trembles at being His*
>
> Soyez la voix du silence en travail—*Be the voice of that silence at work*
>
> Couvez la vie, c'est elle qui loue Dieu—*Nurture life for it's praising God !*
>
> Pas un seul mot, et pourtant c'est son Nom—*Not a word, and yet it is His Name*
>
> Que tout secrète et presse de chanter—*that everything exudes and urges to sing*
>
> N'avez-vous pas un monde immense en vous—*Don't you have an immense world in you*

Come Closer to Yourself

Soyez son cri, et vous aurez tout dit—*Be his cry, and you'll have said everything*

Il suffit d'être, et vous vous entendrez—*It's enough just to be and you will hear yourself*

Rendre grâce d'être et de bénir—*give thanks for existence and bless it*

Vous serez pris dans l'hymne d'univers—*You'll be taken up in the hymn of the universe*

Vous avez tout en vous pour adorer—*You have everything in you that's needed to adore*

Car vous avez l'hiver et le printemps—*For you have Winter and Spring in you*

Vous êtes l'arbre en sommeil et en fleurs—*You are the tree asleep and in bloom*

Jouez pour Dieu des branches et du vent—*Play for God with the branches and the wind*

Jouez pour Dieu des racines cachées—*Play for God with your hidden roots*

« It is sufficient just to be, and you will hear yourself giving thanks for life and bless it ! » You can be happy only if that is the basic attitude of your soul. All the rest must originate from there. Else your energy will be wasted in trying to be different from whom you are.

Exercise 1

Go and sit somewhere in nature and gaze at a beautiful tree. Consider it for a while in silence, not analyzing it nor reasoning about it. Just look at it for some time! Then, pick up a conversation with it : « What are you doing there ? » Listen attentively . . . What occurs to you ? Write it in your notebook.

Or, similarly, look at a cow in the meadow or a bird on a branch : « Why are you here ? What is the purpose of your existence ? » Perhaps they will tell you something important.

Exercise 2

Go for a quiet walk, taking with you the text of the hymn quoted above. Slowly and aloud read out the verses to yourself. Savour each sentence and listen to whatever message the song holds for your soul.

Exercise 3

For five minutes slowly walk in nature while giving your entire attention to your breathing. Do that without thinking, and without looking at anything. All the time just breathe deeply : let the muscles of your abdomen expand first, then those at your waist and finally your chest. When your lungs are full, hold your breath for a few seconds, then slowly exhale. What do you experience ? Do you feel how good it feels to be alive ? Ultimately, that is what matters : you are alive so as to be totally present to yourself, to others, to the world, with all that you are, just like that !

THE GROUND ON WHICH YOU STAND

If you did some of the previous exercises you certainly became somewhat more conscious of the totaly gratuitous character of your existence. Truly, you simply *receive* whatever you are and have. Ever since, and still today, at this very moment you are reading this. You have no control whatsoever of your origine—life daily *happens* to you. If you let this fact get through to you, you might well have a dizzy turn : you literally hang in a void. Not only does our planet Earth hang somewhere in the immense Milky Way galaxy, but so do you ! Do you touch the ground under your feet ? What secure ground have you to stand on ?

Is that something or someone outside you ? Or something very deep inside you ? At any rate, it is an awesome mystery.

Come Closer to Yourself

Since times immemorial people called the foundation of their existence : 'God'. However, that word has a number of connotations and not always pleasant ones, for people imagine all sorts of things about this 'God'. And believers in 'God', have different representations of Him, which changed quite often in the course of history. Certainly in the history of the Jewish people : the Bible presents different God images, and not all of them are enchanting ! And the same holds for Christianity. In case you would like to become more acquainted with this, you could profit from the books of Karen Armstrong. One of her most researched books is entitled : « A history of God : 4000 years Judaism, Christianity and Islam . »

Still, lots of people are constantly in search of God. Or, in other words, they query the basis of their existence. The Spanish philosopher Unamuno once wrote in the British weekly The Tablet : « Those people who think that they believe in God, but without passion in their heart, without anxiety of soul, without uncertainty, without doubt, without an element of despair even in their consolation, those people believe only in a concept of God, not in God himself. » That is strong but salutary language ! For, indeed, we find no adequate name for that which, for lack of a better word, we call 'God'. In his novel entitled 'Report to Greco', Nikos Kazantzakis tells the story of a priest who went to visit an islamic dervish and asked him : « Father, what name do you give to God ? ». The dervish answered : « God has no name. He is too great to fit into a name. A name is a prison and God is free. » But the priest objected : « Alright, but if you want to appeal to him when you are in need, what name will you use ? » The dervish lowered his head and thought deeply. Finally, he opened his mouth and said : « Aaaah ! Yes, that is what I would call him : not Allah, but Aaaah ! » The base of our existence is indeed a great mystery that fills us with awe and makes us fall silent.

That is why the Jews were never allowed to make a representation of God. The prohibition still holds. They built a temple, but in the most sacred area of it, called the Holy of Holies, the place for God was the empty space on top of the cover of the Ark of Alliance, in between the huge two wings of the Cherubs. How significant : an empty space ! And they were not allowed to pronounce the name that they considered as revealed to them (YHWH) but said « The Lord » instead. Islam similarly forbids all representations of God. And Eastern religions such as Buddhism or the Tao do not speak of a personal God. And yet, Buddhists visit temples in which they make offerings to various 'gods' in view of obtaining a favour. In a song by the Dutch priest-poet Huub Oosterhuis, one of the phrases runs like this : « If someone says he is God, let him show himself ! » Indeed, we so wish to verify what this 'God' is really like.

People who do not live a superficial life will automatically—though perhaps not always consciously—be searching for God. But it is not so much a matter of knowing or understanding 'God', but of being in relationship with God. Two friends or a married couple do not know or understand everything about each other, yet they are closely bonded and given to each other. It is the relationship itself that is life-giving for them. That is precisely the marvel of genuine love : people surrender themselves to each other without fully understanding or knowing each other. It is a matter of confidence, of trusting this mysterious love that flows between the two of them. That, in itself, is already a marvel !

When you say that you believe in God, you are really saying that you deeply trust that you are rooted in the great Mystery, that you feel carried by it, that you may entrust yourself to it. And that is the essence of genuine faith. Some concepts or representations of 'God' may help us to do that, but some others merely prevent us from doing so, because they make us draw the wrong conclusions. That is why the mystic writer Eckhart daringly said that we had better destroy our images of God, so as to enable God to be truly God for us !

In a novel by Marianne Fredrikson I found a similar statement by one of her protagonists : « If you have a representation of God, you must let go of it. You can only do God's will when you have no representation of him at all . » In that same novel ('Simon') a father tells his son : « You must associate with God in the same way as when you let yourself be absorbed by a piece of music you like. » In fact, we allow ourselves to be submerged in superb music. Words cannot truly express what we feel then. You are carried along to distant horizons. You do not grasp much but you have an experience of something fulfilling you. You do not feel the need of explanations. You just allow yourself to be carried along. That is exactly the way we must allow God to be God in us.

In the same novel I found this poem that is quite to the point :

What does the sea smell like ?—Turn your face to the storm raging there that carries all the scents of the sea towards you—Fill your nose, your lungs—Start with concrete words : sea air . . . salt . . . .—No, the answer is not in those words—What is the smell of the sea ?—Try it with other words, heavier ones : Force, Freedom, Adventure . . .—These words are inadequate, they restrict the immeasurable—Put the question again : What's the smell of the sea ?—And recognize that this question does not make sense—If you stop asking questions, you might possibly EXPERIENCE the sea.

Father de Mello tells us this story of the seacher for God who comes knocking at the door of a guru :

Is the path of enlightenment difficult or easy ?—Neither !—Why not ?—Because there is no path !—Then : how does one travel towards the goal ?—One does not travel. This voyage has no distance. Stop traveling and you are there !—But help us to find God—Nobody can assist you with that—Why not ?—For the same reason that nobody can help a fish with finding the ocean.

Indeed, it does not make any sense to search for the ocean when you are swimming in it ! You already are in 'God', because God is the ocean in which you float and are carried by. Paul of Tarsus already said so in his speech in the areopagus of Athens : «He is not far from any of us, since it is in him that we live, and move, and exist, as indeed some of your own writers have said : from him we all originate. » (Acts of the Apostles, 17, 27). We only need to become and remain conscious of it. And learn to abide in it. And then you are carried, just as you were carried safely in your mother's womb. You did not know anything at that moment, did you not ? Yet you were safe. Now you are carried by what we call 'God 'for lack of an adequate term.

Exercise 1

What or who is it that gives you certainty of being safe in your existence ? Is it prestige, or power, or possessions, or the support of an influential person ? Is that a solid ground to stand on ?

Instead, have a look at the origin of the Jewish name of God as it is narrated in their Thora. Moses had a God-experience and there he was commissioned to lead the people out of the Egyptian exile. He felt rather shaky on his legs for such an assignment and asked : « But if they ask me what his name is, what am I to tell them ? And God said to Moses, 'I am who I am'. » (Exodus 3, 14). In other words : I will always be with you on your journey, even if you do not know whom I am exactly. Just trust me. Surrender yourself to me, and all will be well.

Do you believe that this is also the case for you ? Is that the solid ground you stand on ?

Exercise 2

Which concept or representation of the divine influenced your life ? How did it determine your way of life ? Have you still the same representation of God ? If not, how did it change ? And how do you feel about that change ? Take a sheet of paper and write a letter to 'God', expressing how it is between you and 'God', and what it does to you . . .

Exercise 3

Perhaps you wish to make use of the Bible now and abide with some texts that possibly express something of your relationship with the Divinity. For example : The book of Job 38, 1 to 42, 6 ; Isaiah 41, 13-14 ; 43, 1-13 ; Psalm 63, 1-9 ; Psalm 61, 2-3 and 6-8.

If you are well acquainted with the Gospels, ask yourself which image of our relationship with 'God' Jesus presented, and notice how often he told his followers that they had not to be afraid but had to trust. For example : Matthew 6, 25-34 ; 11, 25-29 ; 17, 14-20. Or Mark 4, 37-41 ; 5, 36 ; 6, 45-51 ; 8, 13-21 ; 11, 22-24 ; and Luke 12, 13-21 and 22-32 ; also chapter 15.

Exercise 4

Words about 'God' restrict the infinite. That is probably why you don't know very well what to say when someone asks you whether or not God exists and, if he does, what he looks like. But perhaps you *experienced* God in some way. After all, that is what matters in our faith in God : that we live from and in divinity. Such an experience is, of course, very personal and, therefore, quite subjective,—which makes people rather sceptical when hearing about us 'experiencing God'. Still, they would do well to show respect for it.

Did you ever have an experience of the divine, of the 'much larger than you' ? If so, take some time now to abide a while with that former experience . . .

Of course it is impossible to experience God directly ; we can only surmise him in what we experience, in what happens to us. The creator deposited a deep longing in us. In the first pages of this book I invited you to come in touch with that deeper longing. That deep desire is the basis for recognizing the divine character of what is happening within you. If what happens to you is in tune with your deepest desire, you may trust that divinity is at play. Hence it is something that you have to be blessed with, that you cannot produce but only can receive. That is why it is so important that we are open to it, that we are ready to receive all that comes to us from without and especially from within ourselves.

By what channels did you experience something divine ? Perhaps it was something in nature which lifted you beyond yourself. Or it was a work of art such as an enhancing piece of music or a beautiful painting, or a festive religious service. Or it is that deep relationship you have with a dear fellow human being, when you can but feel that love is so much deeper, bigger and wider than what you see or feel in your loving embrace. When your heart exults in an experience, when you feel peace and freedom in yourself then, when the experience gives you more inner power, if it touches you so unconditionally that you can identify with it totally and unreservedly, then you somehow touched the divine in your experience. You may trust it. Is or was there something like this in your life ?

Exercise 5

Perhaps you may be inspired by an American song from the Gaia Mass by Paul Winter, recorded in that tremendous natural cathedral called the Grand Canyon. Can you identify with it ? You can find it on his CD and it goes like this :

> *Oh mystery, you are alive—I feel you all around.—You are a fire in my heart,—you are the holy sound.—You are all alive,—it is to you that I sing.—Oh grant that I may feel you—always in everything.*
>
> *It lives in a seed of a tree as it grows.—You hear it if you listen to the wind as it blows.—It is there in the river as it flows into the sea,—it's the sound in the soul oh of someone becoming*

free.—And it lives in the laughter of children at play,—and in the blazing sun that gives light to the day ;—in the moon and the planets and the stars in the sky.—It's been a mover of mountains since the beginning of time . . . . Oh mystery . . .

And it lives in the waves as they crash upon the beach.—I've seen it in the gods that people try to reach.—I feel it in the love that I know we need so much.—I know it in your smile, my love, when our hearts do touch.—But when I sense deep inside, I feel best of all,—like a moon that's glowing white.—And I listen to your call.—And I know you will guide me.—I feel like a tide—moving through the ocean of my heart that's open wide . . . Oh mystery . . .

WHO IS YOUR MODEL OR MENTOR ?

All the time we notice that youngsters look up to some persons who serve as an example for them. If they are part of a good family it may well be their father or mother, or an uncle or an aunt. Or a grandparent. Often it is a teacher they admire, or the leader of a youth movement, or a religious figure, or a famous athlete or football player, or a popsinger, and so on.

What about us adults ? It is amazing how some people can swear by some politician or go crazy about a football or tennis player. Or feel inspired by an artist, a researcher, a philosopher, a religious personality, a historic figure. It looks as if we all need some kind of role model. Perhaps we are not always aware of it, but it remains a fact that some persons have had a great influence on us, or still have. There is, of course, nothing wrong with that, quite to the contrary ! But it is a delicate affair, for models can inspire us, but they can just as well influence us for the worst.

Who served or serves as a model for you? Consider what kind of influence this model or mentor has on you. Perhaps you can look back with gratitude on that person. Perhaps you have just as well been disappointed with—or even been misled by—certain role models in your life.

Personally, I did look up to some people. I admired my father very much who, as a social foreman, played a constructive role in politics. I have been inspired by a likeable chaplain of our youth movement. But, if I may say so, nobody has moved and inspired me as much as a certain ~~Yeshu~~ Jesus from Nazareth. If you, reader, are a Christian, you know whom I am talking about. Therefore, if you don't mind, I would like to invite you to spend some time with him here, and discover if he can mean something for you as well. But feel free to move on in the book, if you'd rather not . . .

In the previous chapter I said that a deep love relationship with a fellow human can at times become an experience of the divine. For me, the most important channel for experiencing God has been the contemplation of the face, the words and the actions of that ~~Yeshu~~ Jesus, in whom divine features shine forth. Perhaps it is your case as well. If so, I invite you to spend some time now

Come Closer to Yourself

contemplating Jesus. For he is the icon of what your own deepest Self would want to be like. The writer of the Letter to the Colossians calls him « the image of the invisible God » (1, 15).

In recent times lots of books were published that tried to put into present day terms in what way Jesus can be considered divine. One thing is certain anyway: the first generations of Christians have recognized an irruption of Divinity in the person of Jesus and he became their point of contact with 'God'. In him Divinity became somehow illustrated before their eyes. And they have channelled their longing for union with the divine into following the way he showed them. In other words, they considered him as their model and mentor for living a freed and genuinely human life. That is why the fourth evangelist attributed these words to him : « I am the way, the truth and the life ». In other words : I am the true way to life.

Hence I offer you some exercises meant to facilitate the contemplation of Jesus in order for you to recognize how Divinity shone forth in his person, to allow yourself to be touched by the divine dimension of his personality. Is it not significant that he never took the central place of people's relationship with God ? Again and again he referred them to the One he affectionately called « Abba », that is, in his own language, « Dear Dad ». That was the One who mattered for him, not his own person. And that is the reason he has been murdered : because he presented an different representation of Divinity than the one of his traditional Jewish religion. I therefore believe that through him we can get in touch in an authentic manner with the divine dimension of our existence.

Exercise 1

Once he put this question to his close followers : « whom do people say I am ? » And when they gave him a variety of answers, he asked : « And you, whom do *you* say I am ? » If you are a Christian, you may perhaps consider this question as addressed to you. What is your answer to it ?

You can let the answer come up spontaneously from your heart and eventually write it down for yourself. But, if it is helpful, you could also borrow some of the answers you find in the Gospels, if you recognize them as suitable for you :

~ You are the one who makes God known to me : Mt 11, 27 ; ~ You bring me rest and enlightenment : Mt 11, 28 ; ~ You are the light shining in my darkness : Jn 1, 4&9 ; Jn 8, 12 ; ~ You are God-with-me : Mt 1, 23 ; ~ You are the road I can follow in safety : Jn 14, 6 ; ~ You are the doorway to what can truly nourish me : Jn 10, 9 ; ~ You call me by my name and lead me in safety : Jn 10, 3 ; ~ You bring me fulness of life : Jn 10,

10 ; ~ You are as bread that truly nourishes me : Jn 6, 35 ~ You are a beacon of truth for me : Jn 8, 31-32 ; ~ You lift me up from my brokenness : Mt 12, 19-20 ; ~ You are the source that quenches my thirst : Jn 7, 37 ; ~ You are my beloved teacher : Jn 13, 13 & 20, 16 ; ~ You are my healer : Mk 1, 40-41 ; ~ You are the one that sets me free : Lk 4, 16-22 & Jn 8, 36 ; ~ You graft me onto yourself so that I bear fruit : Jn 15, 5 ; ~ You offer me a home : Jn 14, 4 & 6, 56 ; ~ You are the one whose power I may share : Ph 3, 10 ; ~ I may be a limb of your body : Ep 4.15 ; ~ You are the elder brother welcoming me into your family : Heb 2, 11 ; ~ You are the stone on which I build my existence : Mt 7, 24 ; Ep 2, 20 ; ~ You are the one who makes me come alive : Jn 5, 21 ; ~ You make me pass from death to life without condemning me : Jn 5, 24 ; ~ You will never allow me to be lost : Jn 10, 28 ; ~ I may be your personal friend: Jn 15, 15 ; ~ You will do what I ask for in your name : Jn 14, 13 ; ~ One day you will take me to where you are : Jn 13, 3 & 17, 24 ; ~ I love you without ever having set eyes on you : 1P 1, 8 & Jn 22, 17.

Exercise 2

In case you chose Jesus [Yeshu] of Nazareth as your mentor, read a few passages of the gospels in which some of his character traits are illustrated which you deem important for an authentically human life. In what traits of Jesus's [Yeshu's] personality do you see divine qualities which are indispensable for a truly human life even today ? And which of these would you want to cultivate in your own life ? For example :

~~ his preference for the poor and downtrodden : Mt 25, 34-35 ; ~~ the radical character of his commitment : Mt 8, 19-22 & 19, 16-29 and Mk 9, 42-50 ; ~~ love without discrimination : Mt 8, 5-13, Mt 15, 21-28 ; Mt 22, 34-40 ; Lk 7, 1-10 ; ~~~ generous forgiveness : Mt 5, 23 & 38-48, Mt 6, 14, Mt 18, 12-35, Lk 6, 27-38, Lk 7, 36-50, Lk 15, 11-32 ; ~~ humble service : Mt 10, 8-14, Mt 20, 20-28, Mk 10, 35-45, Jn 13, 2-17 ; ~~ putting the person above the law : Mt 121-13, Mk 2, 23-27, Mk 3, 1-6, Mk 7, 1-7 & 14-23 ; ~~ great trust : Mt 7, 7-11, Mt 8, 23-27, Mt 9, 18-29, Mt 14, 22-32, Mt 17, 14-20, Mk 4, 35-41, Mk 9, 14-29, Lk 11, 5-13 ; ~~ No backing away from duty : Mt 5, 1-11, Lk 12, 1-12, Mt 7, 15-20 ; ~~ Honesty, no feigning : Mt 6, 1-6 & 16-18, Mt 15, 1-9, Mt 21, 23-32, Mt 22, 15-22, Mt chap.23, Mk 11, 27-33, Mk 12, 13-40, Lk 11, 37-54, Lk 20, 20-26 ; ~~ Going to the root of one's behaviour : Mt 5, 21-22 & 27-30 & 33-37, Mt 12, 33-37, Mt 15, 10-20, Lk 6, 41-46 ; ~~ Restoring people's dignity : Mk 2, 13-17, Lk 19, 1-10 ; ~~ Going out to people in a healing manner : Mk 1, 40-45, Mk 2, 1-12, Mk 5, 25-34, Mk 7, 31-37, Mk 8, 22-26, Mk 10, 46-52, Lk 5, 12-26, Lk 14, 1-6, Lk 17, 11-19 ; ~~ Refering to the thing most essential in life : Mk 12, 28-34.

HOW DO YOU STAND IN THE WORLD ?

Whether you like it or not, you are part of the world as it is now. You are an individual, but you can't float in existence on your own. You are inseparably *connected* with all the energies influencing our world, good ones and bad ones alike. Is an active involvement with the world part of your vision on life ? Not merely theoretically, but concretely in your lifestyle and in your activities ? The query as to what your attitude is towards the world, implies two questions: *how do you consider* the world, and how are you *concretely involved* in the world. Can you say that you are in, and of, and with this world of ours ? Or do you perhaps think that genuine spirituality implies aloofness from the world, because « the world is bad anyway » as, for example, some sects believe ?

The question is not illusory, for in Christian tradition we cultivated for a long time a way of thinking that was suspicious of the world. Often it was said that we are not really made for this world and we had rather direct our attention and longing to the afterlife. And we said prayers and sang hymns speaking of the world as « a vale of tears » from which we had to be safeguarded or saved. Moreover, in our tradition, we were especially concerned with the personal relationship between God and us. Our attention was especially drawn to wrong behaviour—which would compromise that relationship—and to piety—which would foster it. Moreover, that relationship was based on the juridical concept of an alliance between God and men—a covenant that had to be lived by, on pain of troubles of all kinds. A covenant with the earth was not part of the picture. To add even more to misunderstanding, we came, in the wake of scientific and technical developments, to consider the earth as an object : something we could use and even abuse according to our fantasy. We know all too well what ecological problems this view has presently brought upon us. And, as Christians, we even thought the Bible was our ally for that matter : did the Genesis story not speak of ruling over plants and animals and dominating the earth ? We used these statements to justify all our interference with nature, while the intention of those texts was merely to point to our task of stewardship, of caretaker of the world. In the dominant world vision of the last centuries, a disconnection was made between us humans and the other forms of life, on which we pretended to have full right of dominance. The land, the animals, the forests seem to have no right of existence of their own ; their value is merely seen in terms of usefulness and, predominantly, even of commercial value. But such is not the purpose of our planet. There exists only one biotope of which human beings as well as any other living being are part, and in which all parts influence the others and are inseparately linked with them. In his book 'The Great Work', Thomas Berry writes : « <u>Each being has its own voice, its own expression, by which it makes itself known to the whole world. And each being is connected with all other beings in its own unique way. This quality of relatedness, of presence, of active spontaneity, is characteristic of all that is alive. That is why each living being has the right to be valued and respected, not because it can be of use for mankind, but simply because it exists. Trees have the right to be trees, insects have rights of insects, rivers have river rights . . . And so it is with us, humans : we have human rights. Rights to the food we need and a roof over our heads. Rights to places to stay for our communities. But we do not have the automatic right to deprive other forms of life of their habitat, or to bar their migration routes. We certainly have no right to disrupt the ecological system</u> . »

In another book, 'Evening Thoughts', Berry writes further: « Humans in this earlier period of human development, experienced themselves as owning nothing, as receiving existence itself and life and consciousness as an unmerited gift from the universe, as having exuberant delight and unending gratitude as their first obligation. It was a personal universe, a world of intimacy and beauty. A universe where every mode of being lived by a shared existence with all other modes of being. No being had meaning or reality or fulfillment apart from the great community of life. All that people needed was provided by the surrounding word : not only food, tools and clothing, but also inspiration, imagination, knowledge, and personal fulfillment. This joyous fulfillment was expressed in song and dance. Perhaps we meet with this joyful fulfillment again when we take time to watch our children. Children that run through the grass or paddle, play with animals, or simply splash around in a pool at the back of the garden on a warm summer day. And just as for people in an earlier period of history, those first discoveries of the world constitute for our children a source of education, esthetic experience, and joy of living. Their senses and their mind awaken. And, ultimately, this is nothing else than the universe awakening, discovering itself and becoming conscious of itself. »

Come Closer to Yourself

If we want to be fully and genuinely human, we need to see and live ourselves as part of that tremendous love energy that runs through the universe and works on our planet. Estranged from the cosmos, we cannot grasp nor appreciate our own value and cannot take up our human responsibility. We so easily live enclosed in our limited little world of work and family. Yet, in reality, our dear individual little life is is caught up in a fantastic whole of life. And we are at the same time a small link in the immense evolutionary process our planet is going through. We humans are the latest, least fully-grown, newest sort of life-forms on earth. We have only just arrived and there is still so much to come, and each one of us has to make a contribution to that process by the way we live.

Isn't that a little too grand ? Still, it is pure reality nonetheless. All that exists has a common origine going back over billions of years. The matter that constitutes your and my being is intrinsically related. It originated in one single energetic happening and is still part of that. And you and me and our fellow-man are links in the further evolution of our world : we are called to play a small part in it.

Hence : two invitations you might lend an ear to.

One : Have a look at the way you look upon the world. Do you see it as one great work of art of which you are an element ? Are you a 'lover' of the world and of life ? An admirer and, therefore, a lover of nature, art, science, the variety of peoples and cultures ? If you are a lover of all that lives, the love energy of the universe will flow in you. Become a lover of the world, and all the divine energy at work in the world will shine forth through you. This is so because the ground of all being is generosity. Look at the universe and our world : what an abundance, what a lavishness of forms, all equally ingenuous and beautiful. If you unite yourself with it consciously, allow yourself to be marked by it, gratitude and joy will bubble up in you, and you will be able to absorb and radiate nothing but positive energy.

Two : Be conscious of your responsibility for the world, for the present development phase of its history. Perhaps you think : for Gods sake, what can I possibly do about that?! However, just reflect for a moment : how did our world become what it is now ? As 'homo sapiens' we are not even 100,000 years on our planet, but what an evolution has taken place in that period of time ! And how did that happen ? By means of the contribution of millions of people who, each at their own time, chipped in with it. You and I, we are no geniusses who cause major breakthroughs in the earth's evolution, but we may not loose sight of the fact that our world's development came to be through millions of small contributions by thousands of human generations. You and I only form a small link in that process, but we have of necessity to be a link. That is part of our life's assignment. Whether we like it or not, we do contribute either to the progress or the decline of our world by all that we say and do. There is no neutral position. It belongs to the assignment of our life to cooperate in all possible ways with all the constructive energies in our world. And this also implies that we try to neutralize negative forces, that we counteract anything that harms the quality of our earth.

Exercise 1

Take a seat somewhere in a quiet spot, and become conscious of the incessant, nourishing and enriching exchange happening all the time between you and the world :

~ in your body : pure (or polluted) air, pure (or contaminated) water, solar energy, healthy (or unhealthy) food, refreshing drinks . . . How is that for you ?

~ in your psyche : forms of beauty and goodness that are nourishing for you, insights you gain from physical and human sciences. What a colourless person I'd be and what a bore life would be without the contributions of art, music, science !

How does the world nourish you psychologically and spiritually ?

Exercise 2 :

Consider how you can foster the quality of our world.

~ which interests, passions, talents of yours foster the quality of life in your environment ? Are you aware of the many ways in which your own life forces can make life better around you ? Recall places and examples where that happens because of who you are and what you do, how you can be an instrument for the betterment of other people's lives. Rejoice and feel affirmed by it !

~ Do you deal in a responsible manner with plants, animals, the use of water and of energy ? What could you do to improve in these matters ?

Exercise 3 :

In case you love the Bible, you may possibly celebrate the beauty and wealth of the world with the help of, for example : Jesus Sirach (Ecclesiasticus) 42, 15-25, or Psalms 8 and 104.

YOU ARE CALLED TO BE FREE

Together with the word 'love', there probably isn't another word that touches us as deeply as the word 'freedom'. Adolescents want to leave home so as to be free. Prisoners suffer mainly from not being free any longer. Colonized peoples fought for their freedom. People oppressed by dictators cry out to be freed. The French Revolution was all about 'La Liberté' which was supposed to bring about more 'Fraternité'. And we are all irritated by the ever increasing number of laws and regulations imposed on us by our politicians, which are supposed to guarantee more security and liberty !

I suppose that you, too, long for a good deal of freedom. But experience shows that freedom is a dangerous word, that people understand different things by it. For example : not to be bound by laws—which of course is an illusion—or being able to do whatever we fancy—equally an illusion. Let us leave aside all philosophical considerations, for here we want to speak of *inner* freedom. And experience shows that even people restricted in concentration camps or persecuted in some other way, were able to feel themselves inwardly free : nobody could rob them of that freedom. They could themselves determine what meaning they attached to their situation.

How free are you ? I mean : can love freely flow inside you and, through you, outward towards others ? Or are you still somehow blocked or inhibited ? Obviously, you are inhibited to some extent, for you are but human. But finally, what matters to us, human beings, for us to be happy and make others happy ? Ultimately only this : that love may freely circulate within us and between us. In that case we become what we are meant to be in the mind of our Creator : persons who are life-giving, who turn the world into a better place. But there is only one space in which love can flourish : the space of inner freedom.

That becomes clear when we consider how genuine love is. Father Anthony de Mello did this very well in the 18th meditation of his course 'Call to Love' :

~ « This is the first quality of love », he writes : « its indiscriminate character. Take a look at a rose. Is it possible for the rose to say : I shall offer my fragrance to good people and withhold it from bad people ? Or can you imagine a lamp that withholds its rays from a wicked person who seeks to walk in its light ? It could only do that by ceasing to be a lamp. » But, in order to be *free for* such kind of love, we need first to be *free* enough *from* certain opinions, feelings, behaviours that are discriminatory towards ourselves as well as to others.

~ «Here is a second quality of love », he goes on, « its gratuitousness. Like the tree, the rose, the lamp, love gives and asks for nothing in return. » Indeed, genuine love is unconditional. You can notice it in a child : s/he spontaneously reaches out, just like that. 'Just like that' : that's how love is. Hence, if we wish to be *free to* love, we first need to be *free from* certain prejudices, demands, expectations, attitudes that impose conditions on ourselves as well as on the other.

~ «The third quality of love is its unselfconsciousness. Love so enjoys the loving that it is blissfully unaware of itself. The way the lamp is busy shining with no thought of whether it is benefitting others or not. The way a rose gives out its fragrance simply because there is nothing else it can do, whether there is someone to enjoy the fragrance or not. The way the tree offers its shade. » Love simply is, regardless of whether someone wants to profit by it or not. Therefore, in order to be *free to* love, you need to be *free from* self-centredness.

~ « The final quality of love is its freedom. The moment coercion or control or conflict enter, love dies. The tree will make no effort to drag you into its shade if you are in danger of a sunstroke. The lamp will not force its light on you lest you stumble in the dark. » Hence, in order to be *free for* love to radiate from us, we need to be *free from* coercion and control.

The all important question, therefore, is : in order to be *free to*, what do I need to be *free from* ?

What prevents you from being free ? What is it that inhibits your inner freedom? What are you still chained by ? Perhaps this is now a good moment to descend into your inner world, for you to grow in freedom. The purpose is not that you nourish feelings of guilt or that you judge yourself to be 'not good enough' ! You cannot and will never be totally free, but that ought not to be an excuse for not desiring to be inwardly more free and to work at it.

I see at least three important reasons why we are not sufficiently free so as to allow love to freely have its way in us :

1. Because we are still too attached to certain things or persons and cannot let go of them enough.

2. Because we still drag along burdens of the past, are not yet reconciled with what happened to us or with what we omitted to do, or with some persons who caused us pain during the course of our life.

3. Because we think that we are not good enough and therefore do not love ourselves as we are. I will return to this third reason later in the book.

A first reason: being stuck, being unable to let go, is the greatest brake on inner freedom. We do not know the joy of freedom because, for example :

~ we have the wrong idea about what can procure us happiness : I cannot be happy without this or that other possession, without this or that other person in my life ; I cannot be happy unless this situation changes ; I want to be on good terms with that person, so I must fulfil his or her expectations.

~ our attention goes out to what we do not have, instead to what we already have or receive right now : our focus is on unfulfilled desires.

~ we hold on to this or that other acquired security and think that we will be lost if we let go of it, for example, of certain doctrines, ways of praying, certain patterns of behaviour, certain ways of dressing . . .

~ we are afraid, caught in one or another sort of anxiety

~ and so forth : you fill in the rest !

Such attachments are not reality but an illusion, a fantasy of not being able to live without this or that other object or person, of needing them absolutely. If we were not caught in that fantasy, we would be able to appreciate things and people and enjoy them without desperately holding on to them.

That attachment does not procure us genuine happiness, but only successive passing moments of pleasure or satisfaction—that are not the same as deep joy and happiness.

That attachment makes us unconsciously exclude other good things. Just think how often you were overcome by emotions of anger, depression, fear, discouragement, etc. because you were focused on something you did not have or get, or because you wanted to hold on to something you did have, or you wanted to avoid at all cost something you did not want. Attachment held you prisoner !

The key to freedom, and to the joy of freedom, is detachment. Letting go.

Note that this does not mean that you need to remove certain things or persons from your life. The word 'detachment' can lead you into error. Some people, such as monks and hermits, do follow that radical way. But even for them the simple fact of not having things does not yet by itself give them access to freedom. Something more is required : something interior !

We may fully enjoy all the beautiful and good things of this world. Why else would they have been provided for us ? But it is a matter of 'the way how'. We need to consider life as a symphony of subsequent musical passages within which we move along. If you want to enjoy a symphony, you do not hold on to one passage only, do you ? You taste each melody as it comes along and let it pass by so as to hear the next one and those following. Forced detachment by means of denying certain values, only brings about the same inner conflict as the one caused by too much attachment. You are stuck again in another manner, wereas life has to move on. Therefore, detachment really means not holding on to, not wanting to hold your grip on things or persons, but let life flow. The secret of inner freedom consists in not renouncing anything and, at the same time, not clinging to it, but receiving everything with joy and gratitude and letting it go again, allowing it to pass on. Father de Mello rightly concludes : « When you cling to nothing, when you have no fear of losing anything, then you are free to flow like the mountain stream that is always fresh and sparkling and alive. »

In his wisdom, he formulated four elementary statements :

~ You must choose between your attachment and happiness. You cannot have both. The moment you pick up an attachment, your heart is thrown out of kilter and your ability to lead a joyful carefree serene life is destroyed.

~~ Where did your attachment come from ? You were not born with it. It sprang from a lie that your society and your culture have told you, or a lie that you have told yourself, namely, that without this or the other, without this person or the other, you can't be happy. Just open your eyes and see how false that is. There are hundreds of persons who are perfectly happy without this thing or person or situation that you crave for and that you have convinced yourself you cannot live without.

~~~ You must develop a sense of perspective. Life is infinitely greater than this trifle your heart

Come Closer to Yourself

is attached to and which you have given the power to so upset you. Trifle ? Yes, because if you live long enough, a day will easily come when it will cease to matter. It will not even be remembered—your own experience will confirm this.

~~~~ This brings you to the unavoidable conclusion, that no thing or person outside of you has the power to make you happy or unhappy. Whether you are aware of it or not, it is you and only you, who decides to be happy or unhappy, whether you will cling to your attachment or not, in any given situation.

A second reason for the lack of interior freedom that often occurs is, all things considered, equally a form of clinging to, or being imprisoned in, namely memories of situations or persons of the past with whom we are not yet reconciled or do not want to be reconciled. This prevents us from breathing and loving freely.

It is sad to see how the life of some people is poisoned by things of their past they did not deal with. Instinctively they react against certain manners of speaking or acting that occur today, because it reminds them of earlier wounds they received. It is but normal that we were faced with one or another form of suffering in the course of our life. In our family, in our school, at our work, certain things were inflicted upon us that humiliated, diminished, or even deformed us. But it is a great pity that we have never straightened them out, so as to integrate them in a positive manner. They continue to infect our soul and prevent us from being sufficiently free to face new situations in a wiser manner, even if they return to us as features that resemble earlier setbacks. Everyone of us carries scars. Indeed, but scars are not wounds. Do you have wounds which you yourself keep open and which prevent you from loving and serving freely, or do others always need not to tread on eggshells for you not to feel offended or put out ? This is perhaps an area of lack of freedom that is worth looking at, because it holds out an invitation to grow in freedom. An invitation which will perhaps require that you deal with it, perhaps with someone's assistance.

Exercise 1

Enter into stillness and ask yourself : do I want to become inwardly more free ? If so, in what areas ? And what is it that prevents me from having or acquiring that freedom ? Allow the answers to well up inside you. Listening to your soul is important. And write down what emerges. If you deem this too difficult, you could perhaps browse through the following list, and see if something clicks.

For example, I am not free because

- I want to be independent from others. I don't need anybody's help !
- I want to do everything I wish and as I wish it
- I only think of work
- I want to be seen as important
- I want to have influence on others or on situations
- I want to profit from everything
- I want to be much better off financially
- I want to have many relationships
- I can't be simply be on my own
- I want to constantly acquire new knowledge
- I think in terms of either black or white, have dogmatic ideas
- I think that laws and prescriptions have always to be observed
- I consider certain behaviours as the only ones of value

- I have certain expectations concerning my body, my appearance

- I live in anxiety about . . .

- I still have rancour for someone

- And so on and so forth . . .

Do not merely recognize *what* prevents you from being free, but also *how* it makes you unfree, what it does to you.

Exercise 2

If the Bible is dear to you, have a look at some significant gospel texts and use them to question yourself. For example :

~ Mt 6, 19-34 : « Where your treasure is, there will your heart be also. » What do you value so highly that you sacrifice everything else for it ? What do you worry too much about ?

~ Lk 12, 16-21 : « This is what I will do : I will store my goods . . . » Which expectations and desires do you still nurture and upon which you make your future happiness dependent as if they were the promised land ?

~ Mt 7, 24-27 : « He built his house on sand. » What do you base your security upon ? What insurance policies do you take so as to make sure you will be happy : independence? Freedom of movement at your whim? Prestige? Influence? A good bank balance? Fixed rules? A good reputation? An intimate relationship? etc . . . Those things are obviously not bad but valuable. But to what extent do you make your happiness dependent on them ?

Exercise 3

Prepare 10 small sheets of paper. Write on each one of them one thing you deem indispensable or at least very important for your happiness. Don't reason too much : simply write down what spontaneously presents itself.

Now make a small pile of those 10 sheets in order of importance, in such a way that the least important of them for your happiness lies on top and the most important at the bottom of the pile.

Now take the top sheet in your hands and reflect : if I would no longer have this, what then ? See if you can let it go. If so, put in down beside you on the ground and say : I am letting you go, you may leave if you wish. And then remain awhile with the feelings this arouses in you.

Now do the same with each subsequent sheet of paper. How does that feel ? How free are you *from* that, so as to be free *for* what ultimately matters, namely that you can live in freedom to love ?

When you have worked through all 10 sheets of paper—even if you did not feel able to let go of all ten of them—take up again what you put down on the ground. Reflect : in fact I am allowed to keep those things ! So, henceforth, how shall I keep them without clinging to them ?

This is a rather demanding exercise. You will possible feel the need to pray about it. Jn 8, 33-36 says : « The slave's place in the house is not assured, but the son's place is assured. So if the Son makes you free, you will be free indeed.»

THE TRUTH SETS YOU FREE

We do not speak here of the truth you try to reach by means of the natural or human sciences. True, the valuable insights which they offer may free you from superstition and many prejudices, and you may cultivate the sciences with profit. But here we wish to speak of *inner* truth : about who and how you truly are. You cannot be free unless you are willing to abide in that truth.

When we were children, we were taught not to tell lies. That was good advice. But adults do lie a lot. To themselves and to others. In order that they do not have to confess what they truly think and feel. And that for all kind of reasons we do not need to analyse here. On this point we all are in need of conversion. Not without good reason, Yeshu says in the gospel of Matthew (5, 37) : « All you need say is 'Yes' if you mean yes, 'No' if you mean no ; anything more than this comes from the evil one. »

Surely, that is quite a demand ! For who is easily willing to confess that he has a hard time with one thing and another, that he feels incapable of doing certain things, that he repeatedly falls into the same trap? You should never show weakness : always be courageous ! We have always been taught that we had to become the ideal person. In youth it is indeed important to nurture ideals. A youth who grows up needs to be inspired by ideals and by people who live those ideals. The purpose of proposed ideals is to discover the possibilities that lie within ourselves and which it will be good to develop. We had to become better and better, to make progress, to climb ever higher with sustained effort. In the Christian spirituality one even talked of 'striving for perfection'. But lots of people simply become restless, at times even desperate, when they are confronted with their weakness again and again. And because they never 'reach the level', they feel they are not good enough. Not good enough ! *For whom* not good enough ?

Certainly, that is not what Christians find in the Gospel. Yeshu wasn't looking for extraordinary qualities in his close disciples or in persons he helped. Rather he was on the look out for their weaknesses and inadequacies, for their unsuspected deficiencies, for the sick parts in themselves that needed healing, and that can only be taken care of by selfless love. The only price people had to pay for his help, was simply to bare themselves truthfully as they were. And the people he most detested were precisely those who thought of themselves as blameless : « I did not come for those », he plainly said (Mt 9, 13).

You and I need to have the honest courage to stand in our weakness. As long as we oppose that weakness in all kinds of ways, the transforming force of love cannot operate in us. 'Grace' Christians traditionally speak of, does not readily mix with our power and virtue, rather with our infirmity only. Our inadequacy, not our goodness, is the approach for love.

In his book 'Tuning in to Grace', Abbot André Louf addresses this issue : « The great temptation is our trying to convince ourselves that this weakness is not really our own. Some people even succeed in not recognizing a single trace of weakness in themselves. That is very serious. The life of such people may then appear as very generous because of their great efforts, it will in fact remain forced and rigid : a life in which genuine love will not surge up any longer. They stand on the border of stuckness and are close to spiritual blindness . . . Happily that is not so in most cases. Thanks be to God, we do know our weaknesses, but we do not know how to deal with them. They offend the ideal image we have of ourselves and carry along everywhere. For we spontaneously think that sanctity is to be found on the opposite side of sin, and we count on it that God will show us his love by sparing us from our weakness . . . But that is not the way God treats us. Sanctity is not awaiting us somewhere *beyond* our frailty but right *in it* . . . Only in our helplessness can we be vulnerable for his love and his force. »

And if you observe properly, you will notice that this is also the case in our relationships with each other. Love will well up in others only when we dare to show them our vulnerability and our wounds, as we really are.

With this conviction I am offering you the following exercises. They are an important step in coming closer to your real self.

Exercise 1

Find a quiet place and put this question to yourself : « What is it I never accepted about myself ? »

~ Listen to your living organism : what feelings or emotions arise when you put that question ? Those feelings are significant : they carry a message for you. Allow the answers to spontaneously well up in you and write them down as they present themselves : « Until now I never really accepted about myself that I . . . », and « This is the way I now feel about it . . . »

~ Once you are through with that, i.o.w. when you have a feeling that the most important insights have surfaced, consider them one by one, and each time ask : « What is it that prevents me from accepting that about myself, or at least makes it difficult for me to accept it ? »

And think : what does the fact of not accepting it do to me ? What effect has that on me, and, consequently, on others ?

And if, after all that, you think that you are not good enough, then ask : Who tells me that I am not good enough ? Who is this liar ?

Exercise 2

Already as a child, from early on, you learnt that you had to answer the expectations your parents or educators projected onto you. When you did not comply with those expectations, you ran into the danger of being excluded or punished or being considered unworthy. Quite soon—though unconsciously—, you developed strategies for not losing their love. You learnt to put in an appearance, you put on certain masks, i.o.w. certain ways of presenting yourself or of behaving, although these did not really match with your true self. As you gradually became an adult, you more or less consciously continued to cultivate that in the relationships you made, at your place of work, in groups that you became a member of—even religious groups. You learnt to play certain roles.

Perhaps you already came to see through some of those 'roles' or 'faces' and learnt to laugh at them. But perhaps there are also some of these 'masks' that still stick to you, and which you would want to get rid of, so as to simply be the person you truly are?

By the long and repeated use you made of them, some of those behavioural patterns might well have become some sort of second nature, a kind of sub-character inside you. We all have a small set of role players in ourselves and some of them often take a preponderant part in our life, while in fact we are much more than that. You can, for instance, carry inside you the nice little boy or girl, the shy lad who shuns the limelight or draws in his horns, the sly kid who always finds an escape route, the silent grave, the clown, the rascal that plays havoc, the bulldozer, etc.

Enter into silence and ask yourself which masks you still wear, or which roles you still play, though you distinctly feel that they are not your true self, and even prevent you from being your genuine self in freedom and transparency. If you become aware of them, describe them for yourself. It may even be helpful to make a drawing or caricature of them. Ask yourself whether you wouldn't be happier, freer, more loving, without some of them.

Exercise 3

Imagine you have just died and your family has gathered and are talking about you, about who and how you were. Phantasize about what they spontaneously tell about you and your ways of doing. Imagine that you hear it all, and write down what you think they are saying.

When you have done so, enter into silence and become conscious of the feelings that well up in you while writing all that down. Ask :

~ Is that the real me they are talking about ? How much of my genuine self have they focussed upon? If they didn't, what then is my true self they seemed to have missed during their conversation ? How come they didn't mention it ?

~ remain for a while in the presence of the main feeling you now have in doing this exercise.

~ And if you would now have the opportunity of telling them yourself who you really are, what would you now say about your authentic self ? Put it down on paper.

~ And do not forget that God sees you that way and loves just as you are !!

STANDING IN YOUR TRUTH

It is one thing to recognize the truth about yourself and to accept it mentally, it is another to consciously live and act from within that truth. For that you need a fundamental attitude of soul which the Christian tradition calls « humility ». For centuries monks and spiritual writers have made use of the Latin word 'humilitas'. It is a beautiful word, because it contains the word 'humus'. And we all know 'humus' : it is the ideal feed for the plants in our garden. It is not simply earth but earth for cultivation. We will do well to stand in our 'humus', i.o.w. in the reality of our earthy condition, of all that lives and moves inside us as animal forces, emotions and passions. They hold life energy !

Modern psychology—especially as developed by Carl Jung—shows us that the road to full humanity is not a road that climbs to the mountain tops, but a way that descends into the underworld of the unconscious : we need

Come Closer to Yourself

to become conscious of our shadows and to integrate them into ourselves. Fairy tales have told that for ages past. Just think, for example, of the fairy tale of that Lady Holle who falls into a pit, thinks that this is a disaster, but in fact finds gold at the bottom and surfaces loaded with wealth.

Therefore, it is not merely a matter of standing with your two feet *on* the ground : you need to stand with your feet *in* the soil ! Should all that wants to grow not be planted in good soil ? Humus is not simply earth but soil for cultivation. Humility, then, is the attitude of soul that agrees to be planted in your own earthy reality.

Of course, humus is naturally dark and dirty ; when you work with it, you get dirty hands. Our humus contains all kinds of things. Also materials we do not like to look at. Dark powers that give us mixed feelings and especially the feeling of being ambiguous beings—which we are, aren't we ? Things that can take us out of our precarious balance. But, think of it : does the soil not need to be ploughed and harrowed so as to be able to produce a good harvest ? Without humility, without standing in your humus, you merely deny and repress the disagreeable or apparently shameful sides of yourself, and in doing so you become out of touch with your genuine self.

Life in its fulness begins down there, in the soil. So, it is not a matter of fighting against your nature and of 'improving' yourself by strenuous effort. In some spiritual circles, we still meet people who think that they must 'overcome', or even eradicate, their failings. And then they are disappointed, if not totally discouraged, when from experience they are forced to realize that they are as vulnerable and frail as ever. While it is precisely the experience of our inadequacy that opens us up for genuine living !

And for others at the same time ! Humility is necessary for associating authentically with others. Don't we constantly play at hide and seek with each other ? Games of camouflage ! And why is that? In order not to lose face. While that is precisely what isolated us from others. As long as you think that you must hide your weaknesses from others, you will only have a superficial contact with them : their hearts will not be touched. However paradoxical it seems to be, it is only by standing in your weakness without false shame that you become lovable ! Strangely enough : only poor souls, recognized and accepted as such, can truly come to love each other !

Hence, self-improvement does not consist in trying to keep everything neat and perfect, in reaching a certain level by sheer will power, of which, afterwards, one can be proud in an

Come Closer to Yourself

underhand way. Renewal in freedom is only possible to the extent that you are prepared to live as that ambiguous being you are. Liberation can happen in you when you are truthful with yourself. The quality of your freedom depends on your attitude of acceptance of your inadequacy.

If you can stand in your earthiness in such way that you can affirm with truthfulness : « nothing human is foreign to me »—all the dark and sinful inclusive—then space is being opened for the energy of love. And then some side effects also make their appearance: meekness (being mild with others, without violence), generosity, long-suffering patience, tolerance. All things you cannot produce by will power. They are flowers growing in the soil of humility.

Another side product of humility is humour. Humour is close to humus : ability to laugh at the silly and the amusing sides of our human condition. If you can be humorous about yourself, you show that you recognize that all that is part of you is allowed to be there, that you are only dust and do not recoil from anything earthy.

Still another side effect of humility is that fear disappears. If you are lovable just as you are—« He knows what we are made of », says Psalm 103—you can stand in the light *with* your darkness. Your heart which no longer fears anything human, expands and can make space for the love which is the only thing able to transform all that is human.

Exercise 1

Take a seat somewhere, with your notebook. Enter the stillness and become receptive.

~ Ask yourself : « In what ways do I feel *disappointed* about myself ? » Let the answers spontaneously well up inside yourself and make concisely note of them as they present themselves.

~ Then ask : « What am I *ashamed* of in myself ? » What is it I absolutely want others not to know about me ? And write it down.

~ Finally, question yourself : « Why am I disappointed or ashamed of those things ? And if you become conscious to some extent of the reason for being so, then ask yourself : « Do those reasons I came up with hold water ? Who draws benefit from this shame of mine ? »

Exercise 2

If you are acquainted with the Gospels, read Mt 13, 24-30 attentively. In the first instance the writer of this parable wants to teach a lesson about holding all members of the Christian community together instead of making an elitist group of it. However, you may also understand this parable in connection with your failings and weaknesses. You would so much like all weeds to be eradicated from your soul so as to be impeccable. But that is not the road to true liberation.

Look again at the main passions you became aware of in the previous exercise, e.g. anger, rancour, short-temperedness, jealousy, anxiety or fear, sexual urge, dependencies . . . Do you condemn yourself for these emotions or passions ? Or can you believe that they hold positive energy you could use if you would aknowledge them as part of you and would direct them in the right way ? Do you dare count on the fact that God has something to offer to you, precisely *in* that feeling, *in* that passion ? Are you aware that you pass yourself by if you do not lend your ear to the divine invitation right within those feelings ? Or do you react with self-reproach or self-contempt ? In that case you will give up in discouragement. Or you will cover up or trivialize your ambiguity and become the hypocrite people rightfully detest.

Exercise 3

If you are a Christian and you are acquainted with the gospels, have a look at the person of Peter and Yeshu's pedagogy in his regard: how Peter needed to be aware of his own weakness before he was mature enough to love. Yeshu liked and called him, *not because* he was faultless, *neither notwithstanding* his failings, *but as he was*, frail and inconsistent, and learnt to see it and accept it !

Consider successively :

- Peter's false self-assuredness : Mt 16, 13-23 and 26, 30-35 ; Mk 14, 26-31 ; Jn 17, 15

- Yershu's warning and his promise that he will keep his promise notwithstanding everything : Lk 22, 31-34 ; Jn 17, 15

- Peter's experience of his feebleness : Mt 26, 69-75

- The lesson learnt : love in humility : Jn 21, 15-19

It is significant that the gospels put one single condition for us to meet God in our weakness : that we dare confess it honestly and openly :

Come Closer to Yourself

- The woman who is cured by ~~Yeshu~~ Jesus must first declare herself and not hide : Mk 5, 25-34

- Zaccheus has to come down from his hiding place in the tree and be confronted : Lk 19, 1-10

- Paul : 2 Cor 12, 1-9

- Parable of the pharisee and the tax collector : Lk 18, 9-14

LIVING IN THE HERE AND NOW

We so desire fullness of life. That is why we follow our many desires and dream so much of a better future. But the future doesn't exist as yet and will never be as we imagine it now. Only the present exists. So it is logical that fullness of life can only be reached in the present. Life is being lived here and now, or it is not lived at all but only dreamt about ! Yet, we find it difficult to abide in the present moment and live *here and now*.

How often do we live either in the past or already in the future. Where of the two by preference, depends on our character.

Some people are always busy repairing or compensating for their past. In fact, they are not satisfied with themselves and try to catch up with what 'was not granted them' with regard to knowledge, abilities, study, social position, possessions, influence, etc. Or they live from the memories of their former achievements which they now miss : projects they realized and cannot let go of, because they still want to have their say in them. And so their conversations are mostly about what they achieved in various places in the past. Their mind is with what is gone—irrevocably, is that not ? This way they are also too late for the present and not present to what is being offered to them right now.

Others busy themselves with phantasizing about the future, and even try to give it shape already now—a future that will obviously never be as they imagine it. They make plans, collect data or things for eventual use. They project certain desires or expectations ahead of them and pursue them restlessly. Hence, they do not have sufficient attention and appreciation of the gifts and invitations of the present moment.

"The Power of Now" Eckhart Tolle

Yet we can live a full life only to the extent that we are present in the moment, as consciously as we can. Is it not significant that the word 'present' means both the present time and our presence to it ? The vital question is, therefore, am I present to the present ?

This is of great importance also for anyone wanting to live a truly spiritual life. For the present moment is the only place where we can meet God and be united with him. Divinity is timeless and an eternal Now. As the evolving creatures that we are, we can only think in terms of time so as to give direction and meaning to our further development. But Divinity is all-present and operative in the here and now, every moment again—and in that perspective the word 'again' is again the wrong one !

Dietrich Bonhöfer, the pastor persecuted by the nazi's, wrote from his prison cell : « What we have to stop once and for all, is trying to make something of ourselves. Union with God is simply busying ourselves in the world with what we need to put our hands to *now*. »

That is why the spiritual writer Jean-Pierre de Causade centuries ago spoke of « the sacrament of the present moment » and, in our time, the American psychiatrist Gerald May uses the same expression in his book 'The Awakend Heart'. God's gifts are being given us right now but we prefer to anticipate them in our phantasy. We want things to happen as we fancy them and, in so doing, we miss out on the gift of this moment.

May we not desire improvement and progress ? Of course we may ! But how will that improvement happen ? Simply by way of the creative energy that calls us and wants to lead us onward to the next step of our life, in and through the perfectly ordinary present circumstances and events of our life which we often call 'coincidence' and of which we think that God isn't

Come Closer to Yourself

there or can't be there. Yet, that present moment is precisely the gift that befalls us.

In a fine booklet which I read in my youth, a French Carthusian monk wrote this piece of wisdom :

« There is only one thing we are obliged to : to use well the time and strength we now have. In this way we fullfill our life's destiny, and we have no other obligations. What constitutes a man's value and his development is this : a sharp awareness of what we are and what we do, concentration of our entire being on the present moment.

Once you have understood this and have the courage to live that way, and you quietly gather yourself in total surrender to what you are doing right now, you are living a full life.

Perhaps it isn't the life of a great man, but it is the life of a man, and that is all that matters. To be great or small does not depend on us. What does depend on us, is that we realize our being each moment, and this constant self-realization is what makes us human.

Surrender yourself entirely to what you are doing, without falling back on the past, without worrying about the future, totally present in the present and in this moment of the day that is yours and that soon will no longer be there » (*Harmonie carthusienne, p. 5*).

This piece of wisdom flowed from the pen of a monk—a 'contemplative', as we call them. Is it not precisely what contemplative life—in the Christian monastic tradition as in Eastern spirituality—illustrates in our midst ? Those people withdraw from ordinary life—for some years or always—to do nothing else than to-be-there, in the daily All-Presence, and to live attentively, day by day. If you and I do not feel called to embrace such a radical state of life, we are nonetheless called to live our life in a contemplative way.

When styding in the United States, I attended a conference given by James Finley, a married therapist who had been a monk in the Trappist abbey Gethsemane, and whose novicemaster had been Thomas Merton. He told us the following : « Take, for example, the rain. Sitting and listening to the rain is contemplative. Or, if you are married, simply sitting near your partner is contemplative. The same holds for sitting near your child . . . You are not near them so as to do something with them. No, you simply feel nourished by your immediate contact with the reality of who they are. This immediate contact with the reality of the present moment, is the contemplative dimension . . . Simple actions : washing up, taking a shower, putting children to bed—done with attentiveness, gratitude and receptive openness—are part of contemplative life. »

Are you searching for an authentic spiritual life ? Then this advice is for you an important indication : when you are totally and in a contemplative way present to what is here right now, you are present to Divinity. Living in a contemplative manner—also in active life, therefore—consists in being conscious of the divine dimension of everything in the immediacy of all ordinary days. Children hold a mirror up to us in this regard : they are naturally contemplative, for they are spontaneously and candidly open for immediate experience. You can easily surmise that the fruits of such a way of living are : simplicity, freedom, peace.

You do not have to be advanced in years to acquire that wisdom. Some people are gifted to live this way by the circumstances of their life. That was, for example, striking in the life of the Jewish young woman called Etty Hillesum, who could foresee that she ran the danger of being deported to the Nazi concentration camps. In her journal, published under the title 'The disturbed life', she wrote :

« People tell us : somebody like you is obliged to put herself in safety ; you still have so much to do in your life, you still have so much to share.

What I have to share or not, I will be able to share wherever I am, here in my small circle of friends, or elsewhere in a concentration camp. And if God thinks that I still must do a lot, well, I will then do that after having undergone what others also can undergo. And whether I am a valuable person will become patent enough by the way I will behave in changed circumstances. And even in case I would not survive, the way I die will be preponderant for knowing who I am. What matters is no longer that I at all costs keep out of a given situation, but how one behaves in whatever situation, and lives on. »

Exercise 1

Find a quiet spot and take time to become receptive, possibly by breathing deeply for a few minutes, so as to open up a space within yourself. Then ask :

- Where am I mostly in my thoughts and feelings : in the past or in the future ? Or is it truly in the present ?

- Can I remember instances when I was totally present in what happened then, or what I did at that moment ? How did that feel then ? How come that I was totally present then ?

- What is it that usually prevents me from being totally present to what happens to me or what I need to be doing at that time ? Listen to your soul without reasoning too much and let the answer well up in you.

- What do I need, what must I do, so as to be able to be entirely present in the present situation ?

Exercise 2

If you wish, stay some time with one or more Bible texts that invite you to be present in the present moment. God is then able to do his work in you. Consider how this could become true in your own concrete life :

- Exodus 16, 4 and 14-20 : people may gather the manna for one day only. When they gather a provision for several days, it simply rots !

- Mt 6, 19-34 or Lk 12, 22-34 : each day has enough trouble of its own !

- James 4, 13-14

Exercise 3

What do the following quotations tell you ?

« The future is not something outside of you and where you travel towards, what you strive for, but something that happens by itself. Notwithstanding all the things that happen to you without your influence, it is already in you, because, with all that you are now, with your past history and your previous experiences, it is already determined how you will react to something that accidentally will cross your path. If it is true that the future will happen to you without your interference, then the present moment becomes very central and the only thing that is really important. Your past plays a role in your Now. What is to come is already implicit in the present. Now you have an experience, you feel, you hope, things happen, determined by yesterday and the day before, propelling towards tomorrow, but loose from yesterday and tomorrow because they are in the Now. » (J.R.M. Maas, 'Trees talk')

« There is a deeper way of living, when a person lives every moment *in* God. He does things, but he is totally detached from the success or failure of his actions. His energy is condensed into the Now, and that *is* God. He works for certain aims which are to be reached in the future, but the only thing he is concerned about is the quality of his action now, and that his work be rooted in God. To live that way is to live *in* God, and to live in total freedom, for in this case we are free from what TS Eliot calls : being chained to past and future . . . Such a person is simple in mentality and is a true contemplative, whatever his state of life may be. » (Donald McChesney in The Way Supplement nr.23)

« Formerly I looked into a chaotic future, because I did not want to live the moment right in front of me. Like a spoiled child, I wanted everything to be a present for me. Often I had the certain but very vague feeling that I 'could become something' in future, would do 'something fearfully good', but then, on and off, also that chaotic fear that 'I would go to the dogs'. I begin to understand why this happens. I refused to execute the task right in front of my nose, I refused to climb towards the future step by step. And now, as each minute is full now, full to the brim with living and experiencing and battle and victory and depression, I no longer think about the future. That means, it leaves me indifferent whether I will achieve something tremendous or not, because I have after all that inner certainty that something good will come out of it. Formerly, I always lived in a preparatory state, I had the feeling that all I did wasn't 'the real thing', but preparation for something else, something 'grand', something 'real'. But all this has dropped out by now. Now, today, this minute, I live, and I live to the full, and life is worth living ; and were I to know that I will die tomorrow, I would say : It is a great pity, but it was good as it was. » (Etty Hillesum, Journal 1941-1943)

BEING LIKE A CHILD

You have noticed quite often how free and spontaneous children are. How they live entirely in the present, carefree, trusting. We can look at them with admiration—unless they are too boisterous !—and perhaps we feel a shade of envy. For we, adults, we can be so complicated !

When we ourselves were children, we too were spontaneous and frank. Our elders, our parents and teachers, put all kinds of ideas in our head and prescribed certain ways of behaving, because they wanted us to become as 'sensible' as them. That was even the condition for being accepted and loved. Later we went our own way, but the harm had been done and lied burried inside us. Again and again we adapted ourselves to our surroundings, we made compromises, in order to function 'properly', have our word to say and be taken seriously by others. That was so even in the Church and religious orders : it was safer to accept and integrate the imposed ideas and patterns of conduct, or . . . you were out ! All that has made us complicated. We had to prove ourselves constantly.

And so the child in us went into hiding. It still lives within our deeper self, and would like to become a little more lively, but it lost its voice. It had little opportunity for expressing itself. Perhaps it was even injured and is therefore too scared to express itself. If you haven't done so earlier on, it may now be a good time to let the child in you come out. To become again the child that we still are in the hidden corner of our soul. To have a childlike soul again. To be childlike is clearly different from being childish. Some people like to behave childishly so as to draw attention and be noticed. We rightly deem that kind of behaviour inappropriate. But here we speak of the childlikeness Jesus of Nazareth recommended in Matthew 18, 1-4. He even says that it is a condition for being part of the 'Kingdom of God', in other words : in order that we be able to experience and live the divine quality of love, and foster it around us.

Which characteristics of children do you like best ?

A child has not yet built its own 'ego'. Finding its own identity as an individual happens later, and not without much pulling and pushing. For it will need to use its elbows to acquire a place of recognition. Still, a child has already an 'ownness', a 'Self' that is not like that of the other children. Only, this ownness is as yet unconscious, and radiates just like that without reflecting upon itself. As long as a child has not been fashioned by the adults according to preconceived patterns, it is receptive and open, without being suspicious. It has confidence in life, it is repeatedly surprised at life, it lives life as if it were one great playground, it takes pleasure in living. It is not afraid of showing its feelings. It does not worry about what others think or whether it is right or not to desire and act as it does. It does not shield itself from possible failures, but takes risks dauntlessly. And so on . . .

All things well considered, a child is a living illustration of the gratuitous nature of existence. It is a holy sign of the gratuitous gift of life. Could it be that Yeshu [Jesus] just meant that with his comment ? God cannot effectuate his love in me when I keep on pretending. When I still think that I have to prove myself. If I keep on twisting and turning to comply with certain expectations people have about me. If I don't receive life free of charge without wanting to manage everything. Do you see how this is all closely related to the inner freedom we considered in a previous chapter ? Accepting the life of each day joyfully and gratefully and living the day in a childlike manner, without wanting or having to prove anything, be it to God, or to others, or to yourself. Freely, just like that. Then divine love will flourish in you and thrive in others.

I invite you to spend some time in the presence of your inner child. Allow ~~Yeshu~~ Jesus to bless it, as Mark narrates in 10, 13-16. Let him embrace your inner child, put his loving hand on its head and bless it.

Exercise 1

Which character features of children are most attractive for you ? Stay a while with the ones you can think of and savour their beauty and goodness. Can some of these be resurrected in your present life as an adult ? How could that be done ?

Exercise 2

Do you feel attracted to certain playful activities you could enjoy ? Play can express and somehow celebrate the gratuitousness of life. Play is a symbol of the joyful freedom of being alive. Are you still able to play, to sing and to dance ? Or would you deem that childish ? Could it be salutary for you to busy yourself each day with some playful activity such as playing an instrument, listening to music, draw or colour pictures, play card games, join in with party games. It would be a way of expressing your joy at being alive. Could this become part of your 'spirituality' ?

Exercise 3

Take some time for remembering your childhood. Where and when did you have your happiest moments ? What made you happy ? What could you gaze at with admiration ? Is there something left over of all that, something that could give meaning to the present time of your life ?

Exercise 4

Are you still carrying wounds dating from your childhood ? Surely, you now want to be a caring adult for your inner child. Take that scarred child with you on a walk in your garden or a park, or sit with it in your imagination, and converse with it. Let it tell you what still hurts, and assure it that you accept and understand what it tells you, that it may tell you what it desires, and that it is safe with you because you love it.

Does this exercise seem artificial to you ? Still, with your imagination you do nothing else than what Yeshu [Jesus] did : « Let the little children come to me ; do not stop them ; for it is to such as these that the Kingdom of God belongs . . . Then he put his arms round them, laid his hands on them and gave them his blessing. » (Mk 10, 14-16). Contemplate this gospel scene attentively and join in with Yeshu [Jesus] in doing the same for your inner child.

LIVING IN EXPECTANCY

Is this new chapter not in flagrant contradiction with an earlier reflection in this book, where you were advised to live in the here and now ? Is expectancy not a way of living in the future ?

Not really. Every human being lives in expectation of something good that will contribute to his/her human fulfillment. But how does a person achieve this ? By abiding in his deepest longing with attentiveness. That is why the first reflection in this book put the question as to what you deepest longing is. When you nurture this desire, don't you live in the expectation that it will be fulfilled ? And how do you cooperate concretely with the fulfillment of that desire ? Not by turning it into a craving which you try to assuage with your plans and undertakings, but by remaining attentive to the invitations reaching you here and now. By recognizing invitations to take the next step in the direction of the desired fulfillment. That requires constantly cultivated attention. We need to be totally present in the Now in order to hear the inviting voice, to catch a glimpse of God's Spirit wanting to lead us on. Our human fulfillment is not something that will be given to us later. It is a process happening in us right now. That is why we need to live in a kind of permanent attitude of expectancy.

The Gospel illustrates this strikingly. It is told of Joseph of Arhimataea (Lk 23, 51) that he « lived in the expectation of the Kingdom of God. » Although he belonged to the leading class of his people, he was not in league with his colleagues who condemned the prophet Yeshu, for he was able to recognize the dawning of that Kindom of God in this man, precisely because he lived in expectancy ! Of the old man Simeon it was equally said that he « lived in the expectation of Israel's consolation ». That is why he was able to recognize the messenger of that consolation in the child that Mary presented in the temple (Lk 2, 25-32). These people 'recognized' God's action, at that precise moment of their life, precisely because they lived in expectancy.

Hence, it is not merely a matter of waiting, but of awaiting. '*Awaiting*' expresses the tension towards something promising that lies ahead. It is looking *forward* to, watching *for*. Do you hear the hope in that word ? Children are looking forward to the visit of Santa Claus. It is not a matter of mere waiting: there is suspense in it. Let us hope that we, adults, are also in suspense with regard to the optimal realization of our humanity, which is the purpose of the love energy of God at work in us. Surely, that realization can only happen gradually, but it may easily pass us by if we are not alert. Expectancy is that alertness for whatever presents itself. And this is why we need to be attentive to the present.

We are speaking here of a basic expectation, and not of expectationS. For the word 'expectation' is ambiguous. We nurture many expectations in the sense of the fulfillment of desires we nurture because they seem to hold a promise of greater bliss. However that kind of expectations may precisely make us unable to positively await and receive what is bringing us genuine happiness.

Expectancy has the quality of patient receptivity. What is good for us must be given to us at the right time, and this is why we must be in expectancy without being sidetracked by expectations. The gospel story of the Annunciation to Mary is a striking illustration of this : she too had her expectations, but she has been asked to simply be receptive and to await with attentiveness what was to happen to her. Vigilance and expectancy are cousins !

It is significant that the biblical psalmists often make use of the expression « I wait on the Lord. » (e.g. in Ps. 27, 14, Ps. 37, 34 and Ps.

130, 5). And the reason for this we find in the prophet Isaiah : « For Yahweh is waiting to be gracious to you ; happy are all who hope in him.» (30, 18). Quite significantly : he is waiting to do you good. Hence : you better be alert to notice it !

To have that attitude is not self-evident. That is why living in expectancy is part of an authentic spirituality. We need to cultivate that attitude, for people do not naturally have that disposition. We want to imagine everything ourselves and then make it happen. Often we cannot wait, especially when we are young. Old age should make it easier but then it is often too late to learn it. Elderly people can easily fall into a state of mere waiting, except if they are spiritually mature and can live in expectation, in anticipation of their fulfillment beyond death.

Exercise 1

Imagine a typical situation of expecting something that holds a promise, and feel the expectancy in it, for example :

~ A young woman in expectation of the birth of the baby in her womb. Perhaps you had that experience yourself. What does this person experience, what does she feel, what does she need to be attentive to for the expectation to be fulfilled ? From this example, can you draw applications to you actual state (or absence of it) of expectancy ?

~ Seed that has been sown in the soil and that is now sprouting. The coming of God's Kingdom has been compared to it in Mk, 26-29 and in the Letter of James 5, 7. At your age and in your situation, is there something spiritual that seems to be sprouting inside your soul and that carries some expectation ? Put it into your own words . . .

Exercise 2

Meditate on one of the Gospel texts that illustrate the attitude of expectancy :

~ The expectation of the elderly Simeon : Lk 2, 25-32

~ The receptive expectancy of Mary : Lk 1, 26-38

~ The servants awaiting the homecoming of their master : Lk 12, 35-44

~ The prudent and imprudent bridemaids : Mt 25, 1-13

RECONCILED WITH DYING

What has dying to do with my coming closer to myself ? When I die, there is no longer a self ! I will have disappeared and only God knows whereto !

Today people consider death as something unavoidable that is better if it happens as late as possible : 'In the end'. But is that the right way of looking at death ? Just look around : everything dies and resurrects constantly. Existence is a rhythm of decay and growth. Each day, thousands of cells die in our body, and this must happen precisely for new cells to be able to grow, otherwise we would become a mere heap of dead cells ! Trees perish, but they become compost, or coal or diamonds ! Nature all around us has knowledge of dying and rising : trees have to let go of their leaves in Fall, and appear to be dead during a severe winter. But look : in Spring new leaves appear on them. Dying and living go hand in hand. Necessarily so. Hence it is stupid to affirm that death is the end of everything. Is death really the end of something ? On earth we know nothing that has an absolute end : all that dies can be of use as it becomes new. Ronald Pino wrote the following in his booklet 'Liberation' :

> « Death is not the end ; death is the beginning of something we do not yet know and about which we cannot make any pronouncement . . . Death precedes a part of creation we do not yet know. Suppose death wouldn't be ? There would be no dying and in a wink our planet would become a place where we would have to fight and push and shove to have a spot. The earth would become a hellish cesspool of absolute egotism and war. So, again, we may come to the conclusion that death has a meaningful task for life. In this case, there must be more to it than we can know at first glance. »

When we look at it this way, we must learn to live with death, and indeed so each day. Death is part of living. Life certainly means living everything fully, appreciate its value and savour it, but it equally means knowing and accepting that life is finite in all its aspects and is continually dying. In his book 'Trees talk', J.R.M.Maes writes succinctly : « I am living and dying at the same time, not only in that I am drawing closer to my death via the line of my life, but also in that each day I notice in the things that are happening that I am dying as well as living : a conversation comes to a halt, and you feel the void for a moment ; you lose yourself in an embrace and death is there. It is never far away : life and death go hand in hand. Can I learn to be more consciously aware of the fact that there is constantly within myself that tension between life and death, not as opposite poles that in turn get a chance but as elements that constantly alter in intensity and are always both present in everything ? If I am aware of this, I no longer need to put that one pole outside myself but recognize that it is connected with me in all things and not a foreign concept. In that case I will not need to be constantly on guard lest I meet with death, with my limitations, with the impossibility to manage it or escape from it, with the pain of a separation, with the fatigue of my body or my mind. It is a matter of feeling what is going on in me, so that death is recognizedly present in my life without it hanging over me, because I am free enough to experience my inadequacy. In that case death has no power over me. If I continuously live that way, and death is already part and parcel of my daily living, I will not experience my final death as having power over me. »

Come Closer to Yourself

Of course, it remains true that, the older I become, the nearer that moment draws. Do I repress that awareness, or am I able to integrate my death into my life ? That would seem important if I wish to stand fully in my existential truth.

Joyce Rupp wrote a marvellous poem about that in her book, entitled 'May I have this dance?' Here it is (from page 129):

« With a constant chorus of cicadas / the leaves tumble down / from long, thin silver poplars / they twirl to the ground / dancing the Autumn death dance / beneath the great blue sky.

The leaves seem glad at the going / (is there something I don't know ?) / sparkling in the October sunshine / they fill the air with gentle rustling.

One, then another and another / on they skim down from above / bedding the forest table before me / with comforting crunches and crackles.

This gigantic death scene of leaves / does not smell of sorrow and sadness / rather, the earth is colored with joy / and the leaves make music in the wind.

Why is this dance of death so lovely ? / why do leaves seem so willing to go? / are they whispering to each other / urging one another to be freed ?

May be « you first and then I'll follow »/ or : « you can do it, go ahead» / supporting one another gladly / in their call to final surrender.

I have not yet discovered the secret / of the serenity of sailing leaves ; / every autumn I walk among them / with a longing that stretches forever, / wanting to face that death-dance / and the truth of my own mortality."

To stand in the truth of our being, requires that we give a positive meaning to our dying—repeatedly and ultimately. Perhaps it can help us to let ourselves be touched by some often used expressions and to make them our own :

Taking leave : at a burial service, we often say : he/she has taken leave of us. All is well now. We gratefully bid him/her farewell. The imperfect, however beautiful it may have been, has had its time.—But isn't that so, again and again, in the very course of our life ?

Part with : As I am aging, I am forced to part with many things, because of my deterioration. I must let go of many things : physical, psychological and even spiritual. 'To let go of' sounds rather negative ; 'parting with' sounds better and 'giving back" better still. For I received everything free of charge ; it has been useful in many ways, now I return it willingly !

Make the crossing : in ancient Egypt one believed that, at death, one had to cross a river. In the famous painting by Jeroen Bosch we notice a tunnel through which people go towards the light. Persons who have had near-death-experiences also speak of a tunnel . . .

Coming home : the gospel of John (14, 1-3) and of Matthew (25, 21) make use of that image. So does Paul (2 Cor. 5, 1-3). Probably Yeshu himself must have spoken in this manner, for it is told that the thief crucified next to him heard from his mouth this promise : tonight you will be with me in paradise (Lk 23, 43).

The curtain will be pulled open : we turn around and around in circles to try and grasp something of the ultimate reality, the true meaning of our existence. Now, according to the first letter of John (3, 2), I will finally see what the big mystery is like.

Transformation : I have walked the whole circle of life. First I was formed from a few cells, then I grew up, now I return to a set of atoms that will take on other forms elsewhere. And my personal consciousness which gradually unfolded itself in my mind, will flow back into the Universal Consciousness of which it has only been a spark. Could cremation possibly be the symbol of this : the ashes of the departed are strewn on the earth, or over mountains or into the depth of the sea.

All these expressions are but images, metaphors, but they express an intimate conviction. And if you are part of the Christian tradition, your positive outlook on death can be born from an even deeper insight. You believe in the continuity of your existence beyond physical death, because of the fact that you inner core is divinely constitutive of your true Self. The Bible puts it in this way : that we are « made after the image and likeness of God'. Therefore, it would be utterly meaningless that our personal rootedness in Divinity would be suspended by death. Rather will it become blatantly patent. Saint Paul expresses this by means of a symbol : we carry in us the pledge of the Spirit (2 Cor. 5, 5). We carry in us the guarantee that the river of our life will flow into the ocean of Divinity.

Take some time now to examine how you consider death and how you wish to deal with it. Perhaps some of the subsequent exercises may help you with this.

Exercise 1

Examine quietly what you think about death and what you feel then. Not only about your final death but equally about the many forms of dying in your daily existence. Do you feel rebellious ? Worried ? Afraid ? Guilty ? Doubtful ?

And when you recognize a feeling, consider what it is a signal of : fear of suffering, fear of losing control, fear of desolation, fear of the unknown that awaits you, fear of some judgment, etc. ?

Finally, consider how you react to those feelings. Do you sweep them under the carpet, as so many of our contemporaries do ? Or do you talk them away with rationalization ? Or do you use them so as to better integrate death into your life vision ?

Exercise 2

Remain a while with some gospel passages. Of course, they have to be understood in the cultural context of their time, but which existential message do they contain *for you* ? For example : Jn 14, 1-4 or 16, 16-22 ; Lk 12, 35-38 or 18, 28-30 ; 2 Cor. 5, 1-10 ; Heb. 6, 9-11

Exercise 3

Perhaps you know or can find a symbol of death from nature or the arts that appeals to you as a positive expression of it ? If so, put it in front of you and stay some time with it in a contemplative manner . . .

Exercise 4

How helpful for you can be the following ways of becoming peacefully familiar with your eventual death ?

- Receiving each day as a gift. On rising in the morning, consciously accepting and receiving the painful as well as the gratifying elements of that day. Deciding to live without grasping, welcoming everything, all the beautiful, good, pleasant as well what looks like being a mini-form of dying.

- Recalling the memory of some deceased persons, and connecting with them. You are part of that crowd and are in solidarity with them.

- Attentively being at the bedside of a sick or dying person.

- Gratefully writing your autobiography, recalling all the pleasant and painful moments of your life : your own story of dying and rising.

- Peacefully but consciously writing your material and spiritual last will.

- Asking yourself : what good do I still want or need to do before I die ? And deciding on the spot to do it, now !

- Devising a meaningful burial service for yourself, in which you wish to give adequate expression of your positive integration of life and death.

BY WAY OF CONCLUDING

A dear friend of mine, a lady advanced in years and wisdom, was asked one day by a young woman : « What is important for a good and meaningful life ? » This is the written answer the young lady received ; it is printed here with permission.

« For me, that is a question which requires a very personal answer. We are all different, and what is important for one, is of no value for another. So, I would really have to know you better, for us to reflect and talk about it together. For, when all is said, you alone can give the answer. It is your life that is at stake. In this regard we can say very little about other people's lives.

Generally speaking, what I find important is that a person be able to develop a good self-image, that she acquires a good portion of confidence in herself and the ability to trust others, or at least one other person, enough to dare tell them everything.

As for an answer to your question, answers cannot really be given from the outside. A good and meaningful life needs to be understood from within oneself. Hence it is important that people listen to themselves. The clearest question about meaningful living you can put to yourself is : do I desire it ?

I realize that this sounds rather profane. But the fact that it is to me that you put that question must possibly have its reasons. That is why I will try share with you what has become important and meaningful to me ; in fact, I cannot do much more than that.

I notice that your question touches me deeply. And that the answer will turn around God and Love. Now, you cannot think of any other words that were burried under a greater heap of clichés as those two. So, you won't have much profit unless I give up something more of myself. And that is asking a lot.

All my life I have been seeking to give a meaning to the words 'God' and 'love' that could be truthful and real for me. The answer I have found until now is that I will not know more about God and love than what I experience deeply within myself. And if my answer to your question arises from the depth, from that place in which, as I said, your question touched me, then it will have to be about that. About my experiences of how good life can be when I and my Self live and exist together. Existing together is rather neutral. Living together knows about love. There I experience God.

Perhaps I can clarify it by means of the shifts that I became conscious of : that is, the way it went with me over the years.

I make other and deeper choices about my life. Formerly I thought that I had to put my life at the service of others. Now I know that love for myself (my Self) has precedence over love of one's neighbour. Notice : that is something else than selfishness ; egoism exists because of the absence of Self and leads to estrangement from oneself. We see it in the world of barbarism and violence. I also make other choices when life is contrary. When there is pain, when there is failure, when I am caught in dark emotions or doubts. Formerly I could hardly accept that. Now I choose to let it be as it is . . . but at the same time I also choose to be present to my Self with all the attention of my heart, which I know and feel that it absolutely wants 'the good life' for me. At any rate, my life as it is now, and that it is good. And so I notice that I am more than ever fond of my life. And that I love it !

I feel deeply responsible for the quality of my life and for the choices I make. You should know that the content of my life has always subject to many changes, and it will continue to be so. _This_ is _now_ important for me, even if there is more to come . . . I still mention a few things that are very important for me for the time being : enjoying beauty and choosing to do this frequently, investing in friendship with people and savouring it, feeding my body and mind with good ingredients, going in for processes of conscientization that contribute to clarify my vision of myself and others, building into my day moments to pay conscious attention to life as it moves inside me.

I feel grateful that you addressed your request to me. I needed to search deeply before this answer welled up from inside me rather than coming from outside. Putting it into words has helped me.

May the considerations and exercises offered in this book

have brought you a little closer to your true Self.

That would make me glad.

The author

(I can be reached on magneels.neels@gmail.com)

Angela Josephine Treadway
39D #304 Cambrian Dr.
Kenora, ON   P9N 4A4
807-219-9014